More Praise for The Mentees' Guide

"Lois Zachary and Lory Fischler's book confirms the importance of providing newly appointed leaders the support and tools they need to maximize the learning opportunities available through a mentoring relationship. Principals and vice principals in Ontario currently value Zachary's books on creating a culture of mentoring and her guide for mentors in facilitating effective relationships. This new resource completes the collection and provides a comprehensive resource for establishing successful mentoring programs."
—Joanne Robinson, senior consultant, Education Leadership Canada

"Lois Zachary understands the essence of mentoring. Her new book, written with her associate, Lory Fischler, is another great tool for me as a leader, working with mentoring everyday, always looking to make the relationships more effective. Successful mentoring is not about a cup of coffee now and then; it is a real, committed relationship with clear expectations on both sides."

—Pernille Lopez, president, IKEA US

"A leading authority on mentoring, Lois Zachary writes with the clarity of purpose and generosity of spirit that animate successful mentoring relationships. Based on solid research, her book presents useful exercises and juicy, real-life examples that will help you make your time as a mentee wonderfully productive and affirming."
—Sheila Grinell, president and CEO emeritus, Arizona Science Center

"This easy-to-read, highly practical and reliable book teaches lessons that lead to successful mentoring in cross-cultural and international environments."
—Eric Ng, president, ESSN International Pte Ltd,
Training & Consultancy Services

THE MENTEE'S GUIDE

Making Mentoring Work for You

Lois J. Zachary

with Lory A. Fischler

 JOSSEY-BASS
A Wiley Imprint
www.josseybass.com

Published by Jossey-Bass
A Wiley Imprint
989 Market Street, San Francisco, CA 94103-1741—www.josseybass.com

The materials that appear in this book (except those for which reprint permission must be obtained from the primary sources) may be reproduced for educational/training activities. We do, however, require that the following statement appear on all reproductions:

The Mentee's Guide by Lois J. Zachary.

This free permission is limited to the reproduction of material for educational/training events. Systematic or large-scale reproduction or distribution (more than one hundred copies per year)—or inclusion of items in publications for sale—may be done only with prior written permission. Also, reproduction on computer disk or by any other electronic means requires prior written permission. Requests for permission should be obtained through payment of the appropriate per-copy fee to the Copyright Clearance Center, Inc., 222 Rosewood Drive, Danvers, MA 01923, 978-750-8400, fax 978-646-8600, or on the Web at www.copyright.com. Requests to the publisher for permission should be addressed to the Permissions Department, John Wiley & Sons, Inc., 111 River Street, Hoboken, NJ 07030, 201-748-6011, fax 201-748-6008, or online at www.wiley.com/go/permissions.

Readers should be aware that Internet Web sites offered as citations and/or sources for further information may have changed or disappeared between the time this was written and when it is read.

Limit of Liability/Disclaimer of Warranty: While the publisher and author have used their best efforts in preparing this book, they make no representations or warranties with respect to the accuracy or completeness of the contents of this book and specifically disclaim any implied warranties of merchantability or fitness for a particular purpose. No warranty may be created or extended by sales representatives or written sales materials. The advice and strategies contained herein may not be suitable for your situation. You should consult with a professional where appropriate. Neither the publisher nor author shall be liable for any loss of profit or any other commercial damages, including but not limited to special, incidental, consequential, or other damages.

Jossey-Bass books and products are available through most bookstores. To contact Jossey-Bass directly call our Customer Care Department within the U.S. at 800-956-7739, outside the U.S. at 317-572-3986, or fax 317-572-4002.

Jossey-Bass also publishes its books in a variety of electronic formats. Some content that appears in print may not be available in electronic books.

Library of Congress Cataloging-in-Publication Data
Zachary, Lois J.
  The mentee's guide : making mentoring work for you / Lois J. Zachary ; with Lory A. Fischler.
     p.   cm. — (The Jossey-Bass higher and adult education series)
  Includes bibliographical references and index.
  ISBN 978-0-470-34358-6 (pbk.)
    1. Mentoring in business.   2. Corporate culture.   I. Fischler, Lory A., 1947-   II. Title.
  HF5385.Z33 2009
  650.1—dc22
                                                                          2009011952

Printed in the United States of America

FIRST EDITION

PB Printing

10 9 8 7 6 5 4

The Jossey-Bass Higher and Adult Education Series

Contents

FOREWORD

LOIS ZACHARY HAS done it again. In *The Mentee's Guide: Making Mentoring Work for You*, she and her colleague Lory Fischler have added a much-desired third volume of wisdom, direction, and inspiration about mentoring to round out a troika of books providing essential wisdom and practice. This new book joins Zachary's acclaimed two volumes *The Mentor's Guide* and *Creating a Mentoring Culture*. *The Mentee's Guide* mentors you through the process, and it practices what it preaches.

Mentoring is a well-recognized concept in today's world, but it is frequently interpreted in different ways by different people. When individuals use the term very loosely to describe a variety of activities and outcomes, often without much attention to specifics, they may easily think they are clearly communicating their needs and expectations when in fact these may be interpreted quite differently by someone else. By defining *mentoring* as a relationship, breaking it down into distinct parts, and identifying specific aspects that are associated with effective mentoring, the book provides flexible but direct guidance to support mentees and other readers in their quests to learn and find new insights and awareness.

In 2009, more than ever, individuals benefit from the learning that mentoring can provide as they develop as professionals and as global citizens. Though a massive infusion of publicity has increased awareness of the potential benefits of providing mentoring for youth, especially those considered "at risk," there is also an increasing appreciation in the United States of the value of mentoring throughout individuals' lives. It is this benefit to adult learning that Zachary and Fischler know and impart with such passion, clarity, and precision to their readers. As we move through rapid social and economic changes wrought by technological development and resulting globalization of markets, former employment practices and expectations related to professional and career development have all but vanished. It's up to the individual to determine how to navigate these unfamiliar waters.

Although the documented benefits of mentoring accrue to organizations, society, and to the individual mentors themselves, as Zachary's previous two books have so well detailed, it is the *mentee* in the end who is likely to gain the most from an effective mentoring relationship. Now, at last, we have a guide for those who would like to be proactive in developing a powerfully productive mentoring relationship. Taking the initiative, as the adult seeking mentoring should do in driving a mentoring relationship, is likely to bring more useful benefits more efficiently. This book provides the insights and inspiration for the mentee to do so. Truly effective learning requires adult learners to take charge of their learning experiences and own them. They need to be open to new ideas but also test those ideas' authenticity and power to expand their own knowledge against their experiences and current understanding. Ongoing interactive communication with a mentor helps develop that process.

The Mentee's Guide provides a comprehensive overview, with guideposts along the path from selecting a mentor to transitioning into the role of mentor. Although the guide primarily focuses on mentoring related to work and professional development, its wisdom is applicable to personal mentoring as well. It is comprehensive, accessible, and illustrated with real-life examples from those who have experienced powerful mentoring relationships.

An internationally renowned consultant and expert, Dr. Zachary is well known for her wisdom and experience in developing leaders and her prominent use of mentoring in doing so. Her approach is simultaneously compassionate and challenging, thoughtful and clear-minded. It can help us take charge of envisioning and realizing our futures, leading to better lives, more rewarding and valuable work, and an improved world.

Carol B. Muller
Palo Alto, California

• • •

Carol B. Muller is the founder of MentorNet, the E-Mentoring Network for Diversity in Engineering and Science (www.MentorNet.net), *and served as its chief executive from 1997 until 2008.*

PREFACE

MY CONNECTION to mentoring began before I was born. My maiden name was actually Menter (pronounced the same as mentor), so perhaps it was not coincidental that my work focuses on mentoring. What is certain is that my introduction to mentoring began as a Menter.

My mother seemed to be everyone's informal mentor. She was a leader in a host of community organizations, and people would frequently call on her to share her leadership secrets, bolster their confidence, and support their good intentions. Sometimes she would be gentle, sometimes a bit stern, but she always balanced candor and compassion. Those who were privileged to call her "Mentor Menter" knew that she was there for them and believed in them and the power of their possibilities. To this day we hear stories of how enduring her impact had been and how, in her own special way, she didn't transform those she mentored but helped them transform themselves.

My personal mentoring stories are many. I marvel at how my mentors raised the bar for me, modeled the way, pushed me beyond my personally defined limits, encouraged me to enlarge my thinking, and believed in me even when I was unsure of myself. I was grateful for their time, their stories, and their commitment to my growth. I recall one mentor in particular who always seemed to open doors of possibility for me. She saw something in me I didn't see in myself. To be honest, I was sure that I was going to be overwhelmed as each door opened, but with her support I was able to rise to the challenge, consolidate the learning, and move onto the next one. Before I knew it, I had developed competencies that I'd never imagined. Another mentor stood alongside me as I took on a major leadership role in my community. He was there to support me, help me through the political minefields, and make sure I kept the big picture at the forefront of my thinking.

Although most of my experiences were positive, there were a few that could have gone better. I had no clue then that there were things I could have done, said, asked, and tried that would have allowed me to make the most of my mentoring relationships. I didn't realize that as a mentee I had an instrumental role to play in shaping and defining the outcomes of the relationship.

AN INVITATION TO EXERCISE YOUR VOICE

My experience is not unique. Some mentees engage in formal and informal mentoring relationships—personal and professional—just so they can "sit at the foot of the master." As result, they don't find their own voice to ask for what they need from a mentoring relationship but settle on what they get instead.

The Mentee's Guide: Making Mentoring Work for You is an invitation to exercise your voice with full resonance and not to settle for anything less than what you need. Whether you are just starting out in your career, seeking personal or professional development, transitioning to new responsibilities, retiring, or re-careering, it is important to understand what it means to be a mentoring partner and to fully engage in the relationship.

To that end, *The Mentee's Guide* presents a simple, straightforward practical approach to help you make the most of your mentoring relationship. Although there are many books for mentors, there are fewer for mentees and even fewer that focus specifically on empowering mentees to take an active, creative, and self-authored role in their own mentoring relationships. *The Mentee's Guide* fills that gap. Not only a book chock full of stories, practical tools, tips, and exercises, *The Mentee's Guide* is also an invitation to learning. As we take the journey together, I will guide you through the process step by step, offering straightforward and practical exercises so you can choose what works best for where you are now and where you want to go.

This book is an extension of our work at Leadership Development Services. It reflects what we've heard, observed, and learned in our work with thousands of individuals engaged in mentoring. The idea for the book started when six people approached me after a presentation at Google several years ago and asked me when I was going to write a book for mentees. I asked them what questions they would want such a book to address, and therein lies the inception of the process.

An important part of the process of shaping this book was undertaken by my colleague, Leadership Development Services' Senior Associate Lory

Fischler. Lory interviewed over thirty people of different ages from an array of settings—corporate, educational, nonprofit, and small business. We were interested in getting their on-the-ground candid stories and digging deeply into the day-to-day realities of a mentoring relationship, with all its exhilarations and frustrations.

The stories in this book are based on those interviews and on the experiences of individuals Lory and I have encountered in multiple settings over the years. We've changed many of the details to protect the privacy of the individuals, but the essence of their experiences has been preserved.

HOW TO USE THIS BOOK

If you are new to mentoring, I would encourage you to read chapters one through six before you do any of the exercises provided in the book. This will give you an overview of the entire mentoring process and help you fully appreciate the purpose of each phase. If you've had a mentor before, however, or are already engaged in a mentoring relationship, skim through the book and start out where you are right now. You can dip in and out of other chapters as needed. If you are considering making the transition from mentee to mentor, be sure to work through the exercises in Chapter Seven. If you'd like to dig deeper into the topics presented in each chapter, I've included an annotated bibliography in the Appendix for your reference. Also, I invite you to visit my Web site: www.leadershipdevelopmentservices.com.

My goal is to help you make *excellence* in your mentoring relationship a personal priority and be more reflective about your own role in that relationship. I hope you will accept my invitation to delve more deeply into understanding your role in a mentoring relationship and how you can make mentoring work for you.

ACKNOWLEDGMENTS

STORIES have the ability to stir and teach us. Reading about them often awakens something deep within us that gives us pause to reflect on our own story. Writing *The Mentee's Guide* created its own story, a story enlivened by the generosity of many people.

Lory Fischler, friend, associate, and storyteller extraordinaire—Your wisdom, talent, sense of humor, patience, and dedication enriches our partnership and collaboration every day and made this book exciting and fun to do. Know that I appreciate you and your many gifts.

Story Sharers (you know who you are)—Thank you for taking the time to candidly share your mentoring stories with Lory. Your experiences illuminated the everyday concerns, struggles, and satisfactions involved in mentoring and created the master story for this book.

Paula Stacy, my "book mentor"—You guided me in shaping and bringing to life the story I wanted this book to tell. With your quiet wisdom, attentive ear, and guiding hand you helped me zero in on what was important. I applaud you.

David Brightman, senior editor—We've worked together before, and now again. It only gets better. Thanks for honoring my work and encouraging me to write about it.

Marge Smith—My "critical friend," who always asked deep probing questions and kept encouraging me to bring more of my own story to the book.

Mentors, mentees, friends, and family—You are part of my continuing story. I am very grateful for that indeed.

Lois J. Zachary
Phoenix, Arizona

THE AUTHORS

LOIS J. ZACHARY is an internationally recognized expert in mentoring and leadership. She is president of Leadership Development Services, LLC, a Phoenix-based consulting firm offering leadership development, consulting, coaching, education, and training for corporate and nonprofit organizations.

Zachary is the author of *The Mentor's Guide: Facilitating Effective Learning Relationships* (Jossey-Bass, 2000), a best-selling book that has become the primary resource for mentors who are looking to deepen their mentoring practice. Her second book on mentoring, *Creating a Mentoring Culture: The Organization's Guide* (Jossey-Bass, 2005), provides a comprehensive resource for promoting organizational mentoring sustainability. In addition to books on mentoring, Zachary has written numerous articles, columns, and monographs about mentoring, leadership and board development, staff development, consulting, and adult development and learning. She is the coeditor of *The Adult Educator as Consultant* (Jossey-Bass, 1993) and the coauthor (with Lory Fischler) of *Creating and Sustaining Collaborative Partnerships* (Leadership Development Services, 2002).

Zachary was selected by *Leadership Excellence: The Magazine of Leadership Development, Managerial Effectiveness, and Organizational Productivity* to its "2007 Excellence 100" list as one of the 100 "best minds" in the field of organizational leadership.

Zachary received her doctorate in adult and continuing education from Columbia University. She holds a master of arts degree from Columbia University and a master of science degree in education from Southern Illinois University.

· · ·

LORY A. FISCHLER, Leadership Development Services' senior associate, is a facilitator par excellence. In her role as the company's program-development specialist, she builds client-customized mentoring and leadership training programs. She is also the creator of Leadership Development Services' unique Effective Meeting Model©, as well as a work style inventory that promotes self-understanding and team interaction. In addition to collaborating on the publication *Creating and Sustaining Collaborative Partnerships*, Fischler and Zachary developed a series of Mentoring Excellence Pocket Toolkits.

Fischler is a graduate of Lake Erie College and has studied at the University of Grenoble, Boston University, and Boston State University. She is a Master Instructor for Motorola University, and in 1991 she was the first person to receive Motorola University West's Instructor of the Year Award.

THE MENTEE'S GUIDE

CHAPTER 1

THE POWER AND PROCESS OF MENTORING

WHAT EXACTLY IS a mentor? Because *mentor* is often used loosely to refer to various learning relationships, it is important as you set out on your path as a mentee to understand just what mentoring is and what it isn't. We can gain some insight by considering the origins of the word. *Mentor* is a Greek word stemming from the name of a character in Homer's *Odyssey*. Mentor was an elderly man, whom Odysseus asked to watch over his son Telemachus when Odysseus set off to fight in the Trojan War. We don't know much about the interactions between Mentor and Telemachus; few conversations are recounted in the story. But at one point the goddess Athena takes the form of Mentor and guides Telemachus in his quest to find his father, and the brief description of this suggests what sets mentoring apart from other learning relationships. Unlike a teacher or even a coach, who is focused on helping us learn and practice a particular set of skills, a mentor acts as a guide who helps us define and understand our own goals and pursue them successfully.

Of course, mentors in today's world may not have a goddess's supernatural powers to help us negotiate our struggles, but they have something else, something that I would argue is just as powerful. They—and you, as a mentee—have access to insights and research about what helps create strong mentoring relationships and what helps adults learn and grow. In the past fifteen years, as mentoring has grown more pervasive and popular and as the field of adult learning has expanded, we have learned a great deal about what both mentors and mentees need to do to build and maintain the kind of relationships that change lives.

WHAT WE KNOW ABOUT GOOD MENTORING RELATIONSHIPS

Good mentoring depends on effective learning. We now know that the best learning occurs when there is a mix of acquiring knowledge, applying it through practice, and critically reflecting on the process. This means that the model of mentoring popular in the 1980s, in which an older, more experienced adult passed on knowledge and information to a younger, less experienced adult, is being replaced by a new model, one that is similar to the one that I first described in *The Mentor's Guide* (Zachary, 2000). The new model emphasizes the value of the mentees engaging actively in their own learning and critically reflecting on their experiences.

Good mentoring therefore depends on a reciprocal learning relationship between you and your mentor. Together you form a partnership to work collaboratively on achieving mutually defined goals that focus on developing your skills, abilities, knowledge, and thinking.

To be successful, this relationship must have the following elements: reciprocity, learning, relationship, partnership, collaboration, mutually defined goals, and development. Let's look more closely at each of these elements:

Reciprocity This means equal engagement on the part of you and your mentor. Both of you have a responsibility to the relationship and a role to play, and both have much to gain from the relationship as well, not just the mentee. Although mentees often wonder what the mentor has to gain from the relationship, there is more than you might expect. Mentors say that they receive a great deal of satisfaction from sharing their knowledge and experience. Their own perspectives expand as a result of engaging in a mentoring relationship. Often the experience reaffirms their own approaches or suggests new ones. It helps them reconnect to the people in their organization and become reenergized. As a mentee, it is important that you keep this in mind. If you see yourself only as a grateful receiver of help and advice you may be reluctant to ask for what you need.

Learning The purpose, the process, and the product of a mentoring relationship is learning. Your relationship may be a good one, but without the presence of learning there is no mentoring. By *learning* we mean more than simply acquiring knowledge, which, though important, is but one aspect of learning. The learning that goes on in a mentoring relationship is an *active* learning: the mentee gains expanded perspectives; knowledge about the ins and outs of the organization, field, or profession; an understanding of what works and doesn't work; and, most important, a deepened self-knowledge and self-understanding. The process of critical reflection enables the mentee to transform and apply learning in new ways. Because mentoring is so learner-focused, it is important to understand yourself as a learner and what you bring to the relationship. Because not everyone learns in the same way, it is useful for both you and your mentor to be aware of the how you learn best. In Chapter Two, on preparing yourself for mentoring, you will find some tools for helping you better understand your own learning style.

Relationship Relationships don't occur by magic. They take time and work to develop. Working at the relationship is part and parcel of effective mentoring. It is difficult to learn if you don't feel secure in the relationship. Hence it is critical that mentoring partners work at establishing and maintaining trust. Without trust a good mentoring relationship is impossible. Without trust mentoring partners tend to take things personally and make false assumptions or start blaming. They end up going through the motions of mentoring rather than the process of mentoring. This underscores the importance of having authentic and honest conversations, being committed to the relationship, and following through on commitments.

Partnership In the past, mentoring relationships were driven by the mentor. The mentor was an authority figure who took the mentee under his or her wing; the mentee was there to receive the wisdom of the mentor and be protected, promoted, and prodded. The current paradigm calls for more involvement of both partners in a mentoring relationship. Just as in any other partnership, mentoring partners establish agreements and become knowledgeable about and attuned to each others' needs. Each mentoring partner is unique and that uniqueness includes all of the experience, history, diversity, and individuality they bring to the mentoring relationship.

Collaboration As with any partnership, the work in a mentoring relationship involves collaboration. Mentor and mentee engage in sharing knowledge and learning and building consensus; in the process they mutually determine the nature and terms of the collaboration. You and your mentor each bring your own experience to the discussions that take place. It is this give and take that contributes to shared meaning, and something greater emerges because of this process. Collaboration requires openness on the part of both mentoring partners.

Mutually defined goals It is hard to achieve a goal that has not been defined. It may be defined in your mind but unless it is mutually defined with your mentoring partner you may be working at cross purposes or on different goals. Clarifying and articulating learning goals is critical to achieving a satisfactory mentoring outcome because mentoring partners must continuously revisit their learning goals throughout the mentoring relationship to keep it on track. Without well-defined goals, the relationship runs the risk of losing its focus.

Development The focus in a mentoring relationship is on the future, that is, developing your skills, knowledge, abilities, and thinking to get you from where you are now to where you want to be. Mentoring thus differs from coaching, which is more oriented toward boosting performance and specific skills in the present.

THE POWER OF MENTORING

What can mentors help you achieve? Our research at Leadership Development Services reveals multiple reasons for individuals seeking mentors. Some are looking for a safe haven, a place to go where they can vent or get candid feedback. Others are seeking a sounding board to test ideas. Many say they don't get the support that they need in their jobs, at school, or in their organizations to manage their productivity.

Within organizations, mentees we've interviewed say that mentors were invaluable in helping them navigate the organization and learn about what works and what doesn't in the organizational culture. Many report increased confidence, risk-taking, and competence in key areas. Others report more visibility in the organization and expanded networks and opportunities. Gen-Xers and Gen-Yers clamor for mentoring, and it is a drawing card for organizations looking to recruit them. What mentees gain from a mentoring relationship has a lot to do with how open they are to learning. Let's turn to Kendra's story and what happened for her as a result of her informal mentoring relationship.

Kendra's Story

Kendra had been having a hard time at her new job as manager of customer service at a large retail chain. She sought this job to escape from a very toxic situation in her previous workplace, where there was little communication or information sharing and information was used more as a weapon than as a tool for cooperation. At the time, she had assumed that everything that was going wrong in her previous job was her fault in some way. If, for example, someone refused to share information with her, she assumed it was because that person wanted her to fail. On top of this she believed that anyone in a senior position was probably smarter and more competent that she was. As a result, she became overly cautious, untrusting, and lost all self-confidence.

Even though the culture of the new organization was completely different from that of her old job, she was finding it difficult to shake the old feelings, suspicions, and self-doubt. Kendra had brought the defensive and ineffective behaviors she learned at the old job to the new one, and it wasn't working for her. Although the new job had a culture of collaboration and openness, Kendra assumed that people were withholding information and didn't want her to succeed. Instead of trying to function effectively in her new workplace, Kendra's strategy was to focus on impressing everyone and making herself look as good as she could. To this end, she took a very top-down approach, quickly implementing a series of changes and dictating new policies. She managed to alienate her colleagues and the people who reported to her in very short order.

Kendra was lucky, however, because Sandra, the HR manager took notice. She saw that Kendra was struggling and invited her to lunch one day to talk. Sandra made it clear to Kendra that she believed in her and offered to meet with her regularly to give her feedback and direction. Sandra saw, for example, how Kendra's lack of confidence was causing her to make decisions without consulting and working cooperatively with her colleagues and reports. At one meeting, Sandra said, "You need to take credit for your ideas. I would like to see the day when your confidence catches up with your ability. You have good ideas, but you aren't leading." That comment made a big impact on Kendra. She realized that it was OK to admit to yourself and even show others that you are good at something. She started very slowly and tentatively to switch her tactics. Instead of pushing her agenda on others, she began to enthusiastically and straightforwardly present her ideas. As she did, other people began to see value in her work and to see her differently.

Sandra helped Kendra realize exactly what she needed to do to be successful. She was able to make concrete suggestions for ways to approach meetings, influence some tough department heads, and resolve conflicts with her peers. When Kendra saw the results from her first performance review (which involved 360 degree feedback from those she reported to, worked with, and managed) she was overwhelmed by the praise from her colleagues and direct reports. Kendra had left her previous position feeling like a failure. Sandra's help allowed her to change how she behaved, as well as her view of herself and the world around her. Kendra observed, "With Sandra's help I was able to turn myself around."

Although Kendra was not involved in a formal mentoring program, she was engaged in an informal mentoring process with Sandra which allowed her to develop confidence and success at a very critical time in her career. All this came about because Sandra had approached her and essentially offered to informally mentor her at a time when she needed it most.

The profound influence of a mentor's candid in-person feedback can dramatically transform one's personal perspectives and worldview, build self-confidence, and add to one's professional competence.

Some mentees say that mentoring gives them exposure to people and ideas they would never have encountered on their own. Others find that their mentor's belief in them gives them strength and bolsters their courage in taking risks. Some report that mentoring helps demystify their profession, organization, or job. Still others find the benefit of mentoring a way to jump-start their learning process in new and unfamiliar areas.

THE PROCESS OF MENTORING

Mentoring occurs every day in many places and spaces. Mentoring relationships can look very different depending on the people involved. Although spontaneous and informal mentoring can have great results, in this book we focus on a way to intentionally find and nurture mentoring relationships that will help you achieve specific and satisfying results.

As already mentioned, research has taught us a lot about how adults learn best and what makes good mentoring. The bar on mentoring practice has risen considerably over the years as a result. We now know, for example, the kind of preparation and work that both mentor and mentee need to engage in to develop a good relationship, set goals, work to achieve them, and create a satisfying result to their work together. This knowledge has been shaped into a four-stage model, which I first introduced in *The Mentor's Guide,* and provides a framework for managing the life cycle of a mentoring relationship.

Do you really need a model? Does it seem artificial? Sometimes working with a model can seem awkward or unnatural. If you are concerned about this you are not alone. A number of the people we interviewed explained that although they were initially wary of using a model, they found that it provided them with the fundamentals and a solid structure that made a dramatic difference in the outcomes of the mentoring and helped them derive more satisfaction and learning from their relationships.

The model I presented in *The Mentor's Guide* sets out four phases of the mentoring relationship: (1) preparing (getting ready), (2) negotiating (establishing agreements), (3) enabling (doing the work), and (4) coming to closure (integrating the learning and moving forward). The phases build on one another to form a predictable developmental sequence that varies in length from one relationship to another. These stages often merge into one another, and as you work together with your mentor you may be unaware that you have progressed from one phase to another.

The Four-Stage Mentoring Cycle

Here are the four stages in more detail.

Preparing

This is the *getting ready* phase. It involves preparing yourself for mentoring and preparing the relationship. This phase therefore occurs individually and then jointly. Each partner examines his or her motivations and engages in self-reflection to determine what he or she is expecting from the relationship. Partners then enter into a dialogue and explore these issues together. For mentees, it is especially important at this phase that you honestly examine what you want to learn and how you learn best. The more self-knowledge you have the more prepared you will be to approach the job of defining appropriate and realistic goals. You will be able to come to the relationship with your mentor as a full partner with an agenda of your own. This phase is discussed in Chapters Two and Three.

Negotiating

This is the *establishing agreements* phase, in which mentoring partners discuss details and agree upon goals, processes, and ground rules. The work that takes place during this phase lays the foundation for the relationship. An important aspect of this phase is establishing trust, and to that end it is important that mentoring partners discuss confidentiality. Another issue that should be addressed during this phase is setting realistic boundaries for your time together to ensure that your work is not derailed by discussions of personal issues. Finally, this is the time in which you set up the logistics of your work, agreeing on questions such as: How often will we meet? Where and for how long? What are target dates for achieving specific goals? You will learn more about this phase in Chapter Four.

Enabling

Enabling may be a hard word for you to swallow in this context. Because the term is emotionally loaded, I want to make my intention clear. I use this word to describe this phase in its most positive sense. It is the *implementation* or *work* phase of the partnership. Most of the learning occurs during this period. It is therefore the longest phase. During enabling, partners work toward achieving the mentee's learning goals and communicate regularly about their progress and how well they are meeting goals and objectives. This phase requires much attention and care. There are likely to be setbacks as well as successes. Issues may arise that will need renegotiating. You may find that you need to change the frequency or duration of your meetings. Questions about trust can surface and resurface and should be addressed and resolved quickly or the relationship will suffer. It is challenging, but both mentee and mentor need to stay focused not only on the mentee's learning goals but also on the relationship. This phase is described in depth in Chapter Five.

Coming to Closure

This is the *integration and moving forward* phase. It entails consolidating the learning, evaluating the partnership, and celebrating successes. Both partners reflect upon the relationship, their personal and professional growth, and how they can each leverage their learning. There is a temptation to dismiss this phase as unimportant—after all, the real work is over, the learning has occurred; it's time to move on, right? Wrong. One thing we have learned from our work with mentees is that if this phase isn't handled well (if, for example, a mentor leaves suddenly at the end for a new job), it can leave both mentor and mentee frustrated and dissatisfied. If mentees don't feel good about the relationship it can adversely influence how they feel about their learning. Chapter Six explains how to ensure that this phase goes well.

Different Kinds of Mentoring

Mentoring relationships come in all shapes and sizes and include multiple modes (informal and formal) and models (one-to-one and group) in diverse and disparate organizational types and settings. The following are common types of mentoring:

One-on-One Mentoring

One-on-one mentoring is the traditional and most common model of mentoring. It involves two people working together to help the mentee achieve specific goals. The mentor can be a peer, a more senior person, or a person with specific expertise and experience. The relationship can be informal or formal. An informal relationship may occur without your even being aware of it at first. For example, you may find yourself seeking and receiving advice from a trusted colleague, a manager, or anyone really who has something to offer. A good example is Lory Fischler's relationship with her tennis coach, Ed, which we describe below. Lory didn't set out to be mentored but found herself receiving advice not just about tennis but also about lots of areas of her life. She never formalized the mentoring side of this relationship but continued to reap the benefits of listening to and knowing Ed. In formal mentoring relationships, on the other hand, mentees and mentors are typically involved with a program within an organization. Still, anyone can decide to formalize a mentoring relationship whether in a program or not. Formalizing a relationship would simply mean following many of the steps in this book—identifying goals, negotiating the terms of your relationship with your mentor, and following through to closure.

Group Mentoring

Group mentoring is a type of social networking that honors and shares the knowledge and expertise of the individuals within a group. It typically involves a small number of people who have similar job functions, experiences, interests, or needs and so form a self-directed group to learn from each other. The group is self-managed and takes responsibility for crafting its own learning agenda and managing the learning process to meet members' learning needs. These groups can be part of a formal mentoring program or you can set up your own; this is what I did when I first moved to Phoenix. I had been meeting people who were truly inspiring and interesting and I wanted to stay connected to them. Despite my desire, I was finding it difficult to find the time to connect with them all. I invited them to a first meeting and asked them whether they found the same value in each other as I did, and, if so, whether they would want to form a peer mentoring group in which we could engage in good conversation, share best practices, and support one another. Most of them said yes, and our group was formed. When we met again we invented a peer mentoring structure that worked for us. The format varied over the years. We took turns presenting to each other on our area of expertise. From time to time we invited experts to meet with us. Some years we had a theme and a retreat. We orchestrated our own learning and supported each other in our development.

Reverse Mentoring

Reverse mentoring has become more popular in recent years, growing out of a mutual need for learning. People in senior positions learn from individuals with expertise within their rank and file and at the same time those in junior positions learn from the senior leaders of their organization. It often works like this: a senior person is mentored by someone who has specific technical knowledge they need to learn. That individual, in exchange, is mentored by the senior executive, who offers the big organizational picture and perspective.

Mentoring Board of Directors

In the mentoring board of directors model, a group of hand-picked mentors functions as a personal board of directors to help facilitate an individual's achievement of a clear and specific learning goal. The board has the advantage of providing multiple perspectives and diverse feedback to a mentee by clarifying, pushing, and expanding the mentee's thinking, promoting personal reflection, and functioning as a sounding board. Typically in the personal board of directors' model it is the mentee who seeks out and recruits multiple mentors to help her achieve specific goals. The mentors meet together with the mentee at regular intervals; the mentee manages the learning process, calls meetings and hosts them together with her mentors, and shares accountability for the learning process and achievement of desired results.

Informal versus Formal Mentoring

The model outlined in this book provides a framework for mentoring excellence that is relevant to mentors and mentees whether they are participating in a mentoring program or acting on their own agree to formalize their relationship as mentor and mentee. Thus, those who find themselves in informal mentoring relationships can draw on this model as well. What does informal mentoring look like? Kendra's story is a good example of informal mentoring. Sandra, her mentor, approached her and agreed to give her feedback, and what followed was a process that evolved as Kendra's needs arose. There were no formal agreements or commitments, just two people committed to learning and a mentee who was motivated and open to change. Informal mentoring occurs every day in various settings. It can last a week, a number of months, or it can last a lifetime. The more you know about yourself, what you want to learn, and how to form a good relationship with your mentor, the more you will benefit, no matter how spontaneous or informal your work is.

MENTORING CAN HAPPEN ANY TIME AND ANY PLACE

My colleague Lory Fischler tells the following story about her mentor and tennis coach Ed. It is a great example of how mentoring can happen at any time and any place. Here is the story of Ed in Lory's own words:

Lory's Story

I had been playing tennis most of my life and at the age of forty was on a tennis team. We played in USTA sponsored tournaments and met weekly to practice. One day during practice we saw another team on the courts who looked like they were having a blast. We thought, "Hey, we'd like to do it that way." So, we hired their coach and thus began my relationship with Ed, tennis coach and mentor.

Ed didn't look much like your typical tennis coach, five feet eight, a bit overweight, and scruffy—and not inclined to show us a lot of deference. But what was clear to me from the beginning was that his whole orientation was to my being the best at my game. My game. *And that is where the mentoring began.*

Ed started every lesson with, "How've you been playing? What do you need to work on?" Even when I would tell him about some wonderful victory, where I finally beat someone who had been kicking my butt, he would say, "On your best day, you are never as good as you think you are. And on your worst day, you are never as bad as you think you are." He forced me to stay focused on my goal. Ed taught me a lot about tennis, but more important, he taught me about life. It wasn't good enough to bask in past victories; it was important to keep moving forward and stay focused on my goals.

Another big Ed lesson: One day after I dunked a ball into the net, he asked me, "What were you thinking?" I replied, "Nothing . . . I was just trying to hit it back." He responded, "On every shot, at every moment, you need to go in with a plan. Even if it doesn't work, always have a plan." I have taken that lesson to heart and whenever I feel stuck or stressed, I summon up Ed's words like a mantra, "Always have a plan." While this doesn't always result in a long-term solution or a winning shot, it puts me in control. Without a plan I'm just throwing things against a wall and seeing what sticks. If something did work I wouldn't even be able to identify what it was. With a plan, even if it doesn't work, I can look back on it, reflect on why it didn't work, and actually learn something.

More Ed wisdom: "Play your bread and butter shots." Mine is a down the line shot. He always advised me, "Know what you have that you can rely on. That is what is going to win you games, when you play your best and most consistent shots." In tennis, as in life, it is important to play to your strengths. This doesn't mean you don't work on stretching your game, practicing other shots to use in a pinch, but if you try to make your fundamental game about doing what is hard for you, you will lose games. I learned to know my strengths and rely on them.

Ed was my teacher for twenty years. That adds up to a lot of life lessons.

"Put a positive message in your head," he told me one day when I was working on serving after coming back from shoulder surgery. "Don't tell yourself not to double fault. Instead," he reminded me, "tell yourself to throw the ball higher, or out more or reach for it. Give yourself a positive not negative message."

When I was struggling with my ground strokes one year, he asked me what I was thinking about in trying to correct my stroke. I listed about five things. "Work on only two things at a time," he challenged me. "That's about all the brain can handle at once. Especially your brain," he said, smiling.

I am without Ed now on the tennis court. He died rather suddenly last year after a short illness. But he died living all those life messages he had been passing down to me over the years. And because of him I am living those messages too. He told me, "I have had a great life. I have made great friends, played a game I love, with people I care about. What could be better?"

Knowing Ed, as a mentor and as a friend, what could be better?

P.S. I wasn't the only person who was mentored by Ed. At his memorial service with only twenty-four hours notice over sixty people showed up. When the time came to share Ed stories, after an initial silence there suddenly came a flood of stories of things Ed had told people, what they had learned, how they would be forever influenced by his words, wisdom, and teaching.

Ed's job title was tennis coach, but his work went way beyond coaching. What made him a mentor was what he asked of people and how they responded. He cultivated mentoring relationships when he asked his students to create goals, know and challenge themselves, reflect on their practice, and grow and learn. He nurtured his relationship with his students consciously. It was this relationship that served as a vehicle through which learning happened. Although natural mentors like Ed may not be typical—he knew instinctively what good mentoring involved—the learning that resulted from his mentoring, his effect on those he mentored, can happen anywhere. People can learn to be good mentors and mentees. All that is necessary is for people to come to the process with an open mind, learn about the fundamentals of good mentoring, and put these fundamentals into practice. That is what this book is all about.

IS MENTORING RIGHT FOR YOU?

The people mentored by Ed were mentored successfully because they were ready to receive what he had to offer. In much the same way, Kendra was also ready when her mentor stepped forward at a very teachable moment. She was open to learning and professional development. Because she had a mentor who created a safe climate, she was able to be open with herself and her mentor. She learned how to listen to and respect critical feedback and convert those lessons learned into action. Mentoring was right for her. Before moving on to the next chapters about the mentoring process, it may be useful take a moment and consider how ready you are.

Here are some questions for you to think about:

- Do I have a sincere interest in learning?
- Am I willing to commit time to developing and maintaining a mentoring relationship?
- Am I willing to work on my own growth and development?
- Am I willing to be open and honest with myself and another person?
- Am I willing to listen to critical feedback?
- Can I participate without adversely affecting my other responsibilities?
- Am I committed to being an active mentoring partner?

Although these are important questions to consider, don't worry if you can't unequivocally answer each with a resounding, Yes! Learning to be a mentee can take time. Still, it is useful to go into the process with an awareness of aspects that you might find particularly challenging. The next chapter on preparing yourself for mentoring will give you an opportunity to explore just how ready you are and address these areas of challenge before you move forward.

CHAPTER 2

PREPARING YOURSELF TO MAKE THE MOST OF MENTORING

A DESIRE TO grow and learn is a great start for a mentee, but if you really want to get the most out of your mentoring relationship you have to prepare for it. This is true whether you are in a formal mentoring program or are on your own looking for someone who can give you some guidance. Whatever your situation, if you have decided that you would benefit from mentoring, you may be eager to jump in, find or meet your mentor, and start getting the help you need. But as I described in the previous chapter, the mentoring process doesn't begin with you and your mentor; it begins with you. Before you can engage with a mentor, you need to do some serious and focused preparation that will help you know better what you want to achieve, how you learn best, and what kind of mentoring relationship might work well for you.

Let's look at an example that clearly underscores the need for preparation before we get started.

Ian's Story

Ian had always been very ambitious. As a freshman in college he used to tell everyone that he planned to become an entrepreneur and run his own company. He was impressed with stories he had heard in the media about entrepreneurs and liked the idea of a life on his own terms. Other than that, he didn't know much about business in general and didn't have an interest in any particular kind of business. His ambition was fueled more on image than on knowledge. After graduation he decided not to go to business school. Instead he took a job with a pharmaceutical supply company to get some business experience. He hoped to have a chance to learn the ropes and that his energy, confidence, and brains would single him out for more training and development.

According to plan, it wasn't long until he was approached by his boss's boss, who was impressed with his work and wanted to hear more about his career goals. They agreed that it would be a good idea for Ian to find a mentor in the company. After getting some names from his boss, Ian took the initiative and made contact with Marcus, senior vice president of sales. He assumed Marcus had the contacts, connections, skills, savvy, and experience that he needed. Marcus was happy to work with Ian, and in that first meeting they set up monthly lunches for the next six months. Then Marcus recommended that Ian read Jim Collins's book Good to Great *so that they could talk about it at their next meeting. Ian got the book but didn't read it. He simply skimmed it. By the time his next lunch with Marcus rolled around he had actually forgotten that it had even been assigned. Needless to say the lunch didn't go well. When Marcus asked, "Well, what did you think of the book?" Ian danced around the question hoping to hide the fact that he hadn't done his homework. He could see that Marcus was disappointed in his response, and the only thing that salvaged lunch was turning the talk to baseball, a sport they both loved. At the end of lunch Marcus suggested that Ian research other books or articles about CEOs—perhaps he might find one that would inspire him. Marcus also asked him to write out what his vision for success in five years might look like and bring it to their next meeting. Ian happily agreed.*

Every so often during the next month, Ian thought about what his vision might be but didn't carry his thinking further than the vision he had had since he was a college freshman—the vision of himself as entrepreneur. He asked some friends for recommendations for books but never did anything further with the information. On the night before his next lunch with Marcus he still hadn't done any of the research Marcus had suggested, but he thought that at least he could write the vision. He sat down in front of a piece of paper and tried to put his vision into words. Try as he might, he was stuck. Ian was unable to get beyond the words "CEO of my own company." After fifteen minutes (which seemed like hours) Ian went out to get dinner. When he got back, the paper was still on the table. Ian gave it a glance, then decided to check in on the ball game on TV. He fell asleep on the couch and the next thing he knew it was morning and he had nothing for Marcus.

Ian told Marcus that he really tried, but that he just couldn't see what being a CEO in five years might look like. Marcus looked him straight in the eye and said, "Ian, I think you have energy and you have the smarts. But you need to do this work in order to get the most out of this relationship. Nobody said it would be easy. I will stand by and when you are ready I will be happy to help you."

It is easy to see that Ian wanted to succeed but he wasn't ready to do the serious work that a successful mentoring relationship requires. Researching his vision, reflecting on his reading, and preparing for his meetings with Marcus certainly wasn't a priority. Any sincere effort at research and reflection would have been better than no effort at all. Marcus would have then had a starting place for discussion and could have drawn him out and guided him in the process.

It is all too easy to assume that because mentors have more experience in a particular kind of work, business, or field of study they know best how to help you and to structure a mentoring relationship. Although some mentors in formal programs are also receiving guidance on how to mentor and some may have mentored others successfully, they are not necessarily experts on the most important aspect of their mentoring relationship with you. They may not know how you learn best, how you communicate, or what your vision for your future is unless you make that clear. And you will be unable to make these things clear to your mentor if you have not achieved a good measure of clarity for yourself. The information and exercises in this chapter will help you develop this clarity.

Before you engage in any of the exercises read through the entire chapter and consider what you already know about yourself and what you may need to explore further. You need not do every single exercise; some may fit better with how you learn than others. But it is important to familiarize yourself with the activities and understand, if you choose not to do one, why you have made that choice. You also may also find that an exercise that seemed difficult at one time will be easier at a later date, perhaps after you have had a chance to reflect further or have completed a different activity. Finally, keep in mind that what you do here is just a start. It is likely that as you go through the mentoring process your self-knowledge will grow and sharpen. This is where it all begins.

MENTORING: A REFLECTIVE PRACTICE

Some people may regard reflection as a waste of time, but nothing could be further from the truth. You may be a person who doesn't naturally engage in reflection. You may think it seems like too much work and an inefficient way of using your time. If so, I'd like to disabuse you of that notion and invite you to make thoughtful reflection a personal habit that you engage in regularly throughout your mentoring relationship. It may feel awkward at first, but it is well worth the effort.

According to my colleague Bruce Barnett and his coauthors, who wrote about reflection in their 2004 book, *Reflective Practice: The Cornerstone for School Improvement*, "the meaning of reflection and its value are rarely made explicit in our personal and professional lives." They point out that when you combine hindsight, insight, and foresight you can make the most of your reflective powers. (Barnett, O'Mahony, and Mathews, 2004, p. 6.) Their definition of reflection closely aligns with mine. I define *reflection* in the context of mentoring as the ability to critically examine your current or past practices, behaviors, actions, and thoughts in order to more consciously and purposefully develop yourself personally and professionally. You can liken this process to pulling a rubber band back as far as you can and letting it go. The further back you pull it, the farther forward it goes. So it is with thoughtful reflection; it catapults you forward.

Reflection is an instrumental part of the mentoring experience. Taking time to reflect on your experience and your hopes for the future is critical to the success of your relationship. There is no better time to begin this habit than in the preparation phase.

Everyone has a history of experience that they bring to the mentoring relationship. These are the experiences and skills that have brought you this far in your personal and professional development. They help you make decisions, work well with others, generate plans, and get others involved—the skills that help you play a responsible and active role in your own life. Before you move into a mentoring relationship it is important that you do an honest self-appraisal of your own development and understand your personal strengths and challenges. This way you can better understand not only what areas you need to work on, but also the kind of people and experiences that best help you develop your skills.

The Personal Reflection Exercise

The Personal Reflection Exercise (PRE), Exercise 2.1, is designed to help you reflect on your personal and professional journey. This process of self-discovery will reveal personal insights and deeper meaning about how people and events in your past have contributed to your personal and professional development.

EXERCISE 2.1

Personal Reflection Exercise

1. This is a time line of your career journey. Reflect on your journey and plot the specific milestones and marker events you encountered along the way. Include important challenges, disappointments, transforming events, and so forth. Once you have completed your time line use it to inform your responses as you complete the following questions.

2. Describe three to four milestones that contributed to your *personal* development. Of these, which affected you the most and why?

3. Identify your top three personal or professional successes. Describe the role you played and why you felt each was successful. Which one are you most proud of and why?

4. What were the major personal or professional challenges you faced? Why were they particularly challenging and what specifically did you do to respond or overcome them?

5. How are you different today than you were five years ago?

6. Create a realistic balance sheet of your current personal and professional assets and liabilities.

7. What barriers are you creating for yourself?

8. What false assumptions might you have about your role, your impact, your value, and your self-confidence?

For more information see Cathy McCullough. "Developing You!" *Training and Development,* December 2007, *16*(12), 64–67.

As your write about your experiences, challenges, successes, and disappointments in response to the questions posed in the PRE you should begin to better understand what and who shaped you into the person you are today. Personal reflection will give you a starting point for moving forward. Sometimes knowing where to begin a process like this is intimidating. Give yourself a number of days to work on this. Trying to complete it in one sitting is likely to result in frustration or in a superficial exploration of your leadership history. In this exercise, you will notice that you are asked to complete a time line first. You will want to transpose the time line onto a much larger piece of paper so that you have plenty of room to write in the specific milestones and marker events you have encountered on your personal journey. Use the vertical lines as markers for specific dates and fill in your information at the appropriate time markers.

This exercise starts by asking you for some concrete details to stir your memory. You may wonder at what age you should begin the time line. Of course, that's up to you, but you may want to begin when you were in high school or even earlier, as this is when we often begin to chart our own direction, making choices about the interests we pursue and the people we seek out. Perhaps you ran for student body president in elementary school and lost, maybe you were in a play in middle school and realized that you loved being on stage, or perhaps there was a teacher in high school who recognized your talent for helping others in the classroom. In your adult life, you may have worked waiting tables and realized that you were at ease in dealing with cranky and demanding customers. Remember, you have been shaped by *all* of your experiences, so do not assume that some experiences don't count because what you did was not important. Write down everything you can think of. Don't worry if you can't remember details or if you put things in the wrong order at first. The point is to start thinking about your history.

As the examples above suggest, the remaining questions on the PRE are designed to help you reflect deeply on your personal and professional history. That means answering the questions completely and honestly. You do not have to write beautiful prose—no one will be reading this but you. You just need to make sure you are getting all of your thoughts down on paper. Here are some tips:

- Try to think back and imagine yourself at different points of your life. What were you thinking, feeling, and doing at each of those stages?
- Write about not how you should have performed, thought, or felt but about your actual experience.
- Start with the word *I*; it will make it easier to begin.

- Be as specific and detailed as you can in answering the questions.
- If you find yourself overwhelmed or drawing a blank, stop writing, take a break, and return to the PRE when you are rested and relaxed.

The following example demonstrates how to complete the exercise.

I was recently promoted to my first leadership position and my career in management is now officially launched. When I think back about the events that led me to this place in my life, I recall a small but transformational moment that occurred when I was nine years old. Up until that time, I thought of myself as like most boys my age—a prankster, fun-loving, and always looking for a good time. Then, during a Boy Scout camp overnight, a bunch of us scouts were sent to collect wood to make a fire. Before he sent us out on our mission, the scoutmaster took out a large bowie knife, housed in a leather sheath. Six of us huddled around that knife, staring at it like it was precious treasure or a deadly snake, or both. Our scoutmaster said, "I am going to give this knife to one of you to use to cut kindling. But it is dangerous, and it needs to be handled by someone who has shown me leadership and good judgment." And then an amazing thing happened! He handed the knife to me. I was stunned. I was overwhelmed. I was proud. I was in awe. And I was transformed from that moment. I had never seen myself as a leader, as responsible, as particularly special. But at that moment, someone saw something in me that I hadn't seen. And from that moment on, I wanted to be the person who deserved to carry the knife.

CREATING A PERSONAL VISION

It is hard to arrive at a destination if you don't know where you have been and even harder if you don't know where you are going. Embarking on a mentoring journey requires a sense of the destination and end goal. It will expedite your mentoring relationship and help focus your conversation if you have done the important work of exploring your own destination. The activity of creating a personal vision has proven helpful to mentees who are about to begin a mentoring relationship. Those who craft a personal vision are significantly more effective in their jobs and more likely to achieve their financial and professional goals than those who do not. It has been said, "If you can imagine it, you can achieve it. If you can dream it, you can become it." I invite you to think about the possibilities that lie ahead of you and imagine yourself realizing your full potential.

Have you ever, for example, closed your eyes and imagined yourself in another place doing something very different? Have you at some time wished you were in a different position—working in TV broadcasting, helping relief workers in a refugee camp, managing your department instead of following orders? Part of visioning is thinking about yourself in your ideal, optimal, preferred state. It focuses not where you are now but where you would like to be if the stars aligned and your best hopes and dreams were realized. A personal vision statement is not about winning the lottery or wishing that your divorced parents would reunite. It doesn't rely on outside people, events, or magic. Instead, a personal vision statement is an expression of the future you want to have. It is a vivid description and a detailed picture of your life fulfilled. It articulates the values to which you ascribe and that guide your life. Creating a personal vision statement is a risk-taking activity. You are pushing your personal envelope and imaging yourself out of your comfort zone doing something that so far has only resided in the back of your mind. By putting your vision into words you are bringing it center stage. A personal vision statement is also an act of leadership. Leaders align their behavior with their vision. They create a concrete view of the world they want to create and then work to get others on board. In leadership, the vision may be directed at the organization. In this case, it is personal.

How to Get Started

Start by getting into a relaxed state and finding a stress-free, distraction-free environment. Allow yourself at least thirty minutes of uninterrupted time to work at completing this activity. Get in front of your computer or use a notebook or pad of paper. Begin by thinking of yourself, five years from now, in a highly fulfilled and happy state. Allow yourself to dream. Remember, anything is possible, so don't censor your thoughts as they surface. To help you focus your thinking and develop a clear vision, answer the following questions. Because you are putting yourself in your future, answer the questions in the present tense:

- What job are you doing?
- How are you contributing to the success of your organization or the enterprise you are engaged in?
- What are people saying about your performance? Your contribution?
- What impact are you having on the people around you?
- In what ways have you grown, developed, or raised your skill level?

Stretch your thinking and don't settle for easily accomplished goals. If you are trying for a new position, envisioning yourself getting it and functioning in it is not enough of a reach. What's next after that? What would really "knock your socks off"? Make sure you stay positive and optimistic. If you have a smile on your face while you are writing, you are probably on the right path. Try to suspend your internal critic and your modesty as you work on your vision. This is a time to stretch. Be as descriptive as is necessary for you to see yourself in your mind's eye living the vision. Play your vision out to the end. Where does it lead? What is the legacy that you will leave behind?

Once you have fully answered the questions the next step is to put it all together into a clear statement of your vision of the future. On a separate piece of paper describe your vision as if it were real today. The purpose of this statement is to communicate to yourself and others as clearly as possible what you will be doing and what that will be like. Using the present tense is a way of giving the future an immediacy and reality. The following is an example of a vision statement. Notice that it is written in the present tense and reads as though the person writing it is actually doing the job she envisions.

Mary's Vision Statement

I arrive early to work this morning and I am eager to get started. I am working with two former coworkers at a graphic design firm doing lots of creative and interesting projects. The firm has grown in size and reputation since I have been there and I like to think that, in part, it is due to what I have contributed to building a talented team in the firm. I love the diversity of ideas that float around the table as part of the creative process and being encouraged to just "go for it" without any restrictions. I am much more open to learning and, as a result, welcome any feedback that is given to me. I am contributing to the organization by being very collaborative in my approach and bringing people into the process from idea conception to execution. I've gotten plenty of kudos from my boss and coworkers about the quality of projects delivered and my ability to meet deadlines. I feel valued and appreciated. Many clients specifically ask for my services on their project and I have developed a faithful following. I am relaxed and happy—a big change from where I was five years ago—and amaze myself with how well I am able balance work and family. I am taking creative writing courses at a community college near my home and several of my short stories are being published.

At some point, either before or after you have written up your formal statement, you will want to consult the checklist in Exercise 2.2.

EXERCISE 2.2

Beginning with the End in Mind: Visioning Checklist

Visioning Criteria	Yes	No
Will my vision require me to stretch to achieve it?		
Will I need to expand my skills and competencies?		
Does my vision excite me?		
Does my vision support my values and beliefs?		
Is my vision aligned with my development goals?		
Can I picture my vision fulfilled in very concrete terms?		
If I were to describe my vision to someone else would they be able see it?		
Will achieving the vision make me feel proud?		
Is my vision clear and to the point?		
Does my vision express hope and optimism?		
Does my vision include empowering words?		

Answering the questions in Exercise 2.2 about your vision will help you make sure that it will be truly helpful as a tool to guide you in the mentoring process. Getting feedback from friends and coworkers on your vision will also be helpful. I encourage you to talk about it and test out how it feels to speak about your goals and dream out loud. When you get feedback, listen carefully and with an open mind. Let's look at Mary's vision and see whether it meets the criteria set forth in the checklist.

Mary's vision would certainly require her to stretch. She might even need to change jobs and expand her skills in order to achieve this vision. She is obviously excited about it. We don't know for sure that her vision is aligned with her development goals, but we have the sense that it is. Her vision is realistic and she has a clear picture of what that would be like. In fact, we can see it clearly from her description. Her phrases "eager to get to work," "contributing to the organization," "getting kudos," "amaze myself," and "happy" are empowering expressions filled with hope and optimism.

One of the most important things a mentor can help you do is work toward your vision. Doing so productively, however, requires that you understand the skills required to fulfill this vision, your current level of competency in each skill, and what you need to do to improve or acquire these skills. In other words, what are the gaps in your skills that need to be addressed before you can achieve what you want to achieve? Exercise 2.3 below will help you engage in analyzing these gaps.

To help you understand this process, let's take another look at the example of Mary. Mary was excited about the person she described in her vision but she also knew that she had to get out of her own way to arrive there. She interviewed a few of her colleagues and her boss about what they saw as critical success factors for realizing her vision. As a result, she was able to identify seven competencies that she needed to develop. In Exhibit 2.1 you will find a sample of Mary's Gap Analysis that provides a list of these competencies.

Technical expertise was the first on Mary's list. She was pleased that she could rate herself high on that competency but realized that it was probably the easiest of the seven for her to develop. She was relieved as well that client relationships was fairly high but recognized that she needed to bring a stronger voice to the table when she met with clients and do more selling of ideas rather than receiving instructions. She also realized that she had work to do in terms of risk taking, initiative, confidence, time management, and conflict management, all of which had been in her way for a long time.

EXERCISE 2.3

From Vision to Goal Setting: Gap Analysis Exercise

Instructions: What gaps exist between your vision and current competency?

Competency	Current Competency Level (low) 1–5 (high)	Competencies to Be Developed (Those you want to work on)

EXHIBIT 2.1

From Vision to Goal Setting: Mary's Gap Analysis

Instructions: What gaps exist between your vision and current competency?

Competency	Current Competency Level (low) 1–5 (high)	Competencies to Be Developed("*" Those Mary wanted to work on)
Technical expertise	4	* Master the ABC 6.2 program
Client relationships	3.5	* Selling ideas rather than waiting for clients' reaction
Risk taking	2.5	* Tolerating mistakes and being out of my comfort zone
Initiative	2.5	Planning and leading a project
Confidence	2.5	Not second guessing myself and being comfortable with decision making
Time management	2	Planning the project milestones and sticking to schedules; giving up on perfectionism to meet timelines
Conflict management	2	Recognizing that we both have perspectives and it isn't personal if others see it differently. Being able to raise issues, not take positions, without fearing the conflict

As you move forward before or during your mentoring relationship, hone your vision; assess the competencies you have and the competencies you need to achieve that vision; and then identify goals that you want to work on. Your personal analysis of strengths and weaknesses and gaps in competencies is excellent preparation for your opening conversation with your mentor.

What If You Don't Have a Vision?

Coming up with a vision may be very challenging. Not everyone has a clear sense of the possibilities that exist and what it might feel like to work in a particular job. Remember Ian, who was stuck when he couldn't envision what it might be like to be a CEO of his own company? What Ian needed to do was to persevere and begin the process of thinking seriously about his vision. Even though you may feel stuck it is important that you begin the process. Your vision isn't a contract, it isn't a promise, and it isn't necessarily realistic. It is simply a point to begin a conversation with yourself and with your mentor. You might want to "try on" various visions and see what fits. Don't worry about details at first, just think about yourself at work. Are you traveling and going to meetings? Are you collaborating with various people one on one or are you in front of a group giving a presentation? Maybe you are working quietly at home by yourself and taking time to go for walks or water your garden. You may not be ready to articulate a full-fledged professional vision, but there is probably something that you can put on paper about your hopes and dreams that will give you and your mentor a starting point.

HOW YOU FUNCTION IN A MENTORING RELATIONSHIP

Another level of analysis that should be completed before moving into a mentoring relationship focuses on your previous experience being mentored. In some way all of us have had this experience, even if at the time we didn't consciously look at it as mentoring. If you look back at your life (again, consider the time line you created in your PRE) there are certainly people who gave you guidance, advice, or support. This might have been a grandparent or other family member; a teacher or coach, such as Ed, Lory's tennis coach, in Chapter One; or a boss or colleague.

Insights from Experience

Consider the following four questions to help you reflect on previous mentoring relationships or relationships you've had with others who have guided, supported, and strengthened you. Reflecting on these questions should reveal some powerful insights about what worked in the relationships, what could have worked better, and why.

1. What were the most satisfying aspects of those relationships and why?

2. What did you learn about being in a mentoring relationship?

3. What did it require from you to make the most of the relationship?

4. What lessons will you carry forward for your present mentoring relationship?

You may discover, for example, that you had a hard time asking for help or showing weakness and, on reflection, you realize you could have gotten much more from the experience had you been willing to reveal more. Or you may notice that the person who was the most helpful to you had a certain way of giving you feedback. Perhaps he used humor or was very direct and frank. Maybe you responded best to direct advice or perhaps you got the most from someone who was a great listener. These kinds of insights can help you make decisions about who would be a good mentor for you and can also be shared with a new mentor to help you both find ways to work together effectively.

Mentee Skills

Being involved in a mentoring relationship isn't something you do once and then you are launched. It is something that you learn to do and then learn to do better. You will learn as your relationship unfolds by honing your skills and thus getting more and more out of it.

Your mentoring experience can be qualitatively better if you possess and use specific skills. Prepare for the relationship by understanding what these skills are, how they can affect the mentoring process, and what your competency level is with each. Exercise 2.4 lists these mentoring skills and asks you to identify your proficiency level and what you need to work on for each. It is important to consider all of these skills so you don't simply rely on your areas of strength, using the skills you already have or are best at while neglecting others. Knowing which of your skills are weak and targeting them can help you grow in ways that are surprising as well as enormously beneficial. Before you do this exercise, let's take a moment to look closely at each of these ten skills. These are the some of the essential skills for mentees, and ones that mentees find the most challenging.

Let's examine each of the skills in Exercise 2.4 in more detail.

EXERCISE 2.4

Mentee Skill Inventory

Instructions: Evaluate your proficiency on the mentee skills listed below. Once you have identified what you need to work on (medium and low), look for ways to develop your skills. You may want to discuss your assessment with your mentor and use it to set some personal goals. Evaluate your progress as you work on increasing your proficiency level.

Number	Skill	High	Medium	Low	Developing My Skills
1.	Giving and receiving feedback				
2.	Self-directed learning				
3.	Building relationships				
4.	Communication				
5.	Goal setting				
6.	Effective listening				
7.	Follow-through				
8.	Reflection				
9.	Initiative				
10.	Valuing differences				

1. *Giving and receiving feedback.* Being able to ask for, give, receive, act on, and accept feedback effectively is a practiced skill. Most people are better at giving feedback than they are at asking for, receiving, and accepting it. You will need to use your feedback skills, especially your ability to receive, accept, and act on feedback, to get the maximum benefit from the mentoring relationship. What feedback challenges do you typically face?

2. *Self-directed learning.* At one time mentoring was based on the "sage on the stage" concept, meaning that the relationship was mentor-driven. That paradigm has shifted over time. Today, mentee and mentor collaborate to meet the mentee's learning goals. In practical terms this means that, as the mentee, you are in charge of your own learning. Together with your mentor, you define your specific learning needs, identify what it is you want to learn, formulate learning goals, identify relevant learning resources, select and implement learning strategies, and evaluate the learning that results. How proficient are you as a self-directed learner?

3. *Building relationships.* There is no magic wand that you can wave to build a mentoring relationship. It takes time to get to know one another and so it develops over time. As a mentee, you need to be authentic and open, sharing yourself and your story so that your mentor can get to know you. You need to come to the relationship with curiosity and commitment about your mentoring partner and be steadfast in working on the partnership. Does relationship building come naturally to you or do you need to work at it?

4. *Communication.* Effective communication is critical to successful mentoring, just as it is in any relationship. Good communication depends on building up a trust account so that you have enough trust deposits to encourage open and authentic communication. People who are good at this skill continuously check for understanding and clearly say what they mean and mean what they say. How well do you communicate?

5. *Goal setting.* Since setting and working toward completion of learning goals is the focus of the mentoring relationship, this is a vital skill to develop. Remember that these are your goals, not your mentor's. Your mentor can help you crystallize and clarify them, but at the end of the day they are your goals; you own them. You and your mentoring partner must each understand them since you will be measuring your progress against them. Your goals will need to be specific, measurable, action oriented, realistic, and timely. Does goal setting come easily to you?

6. *Effective listening.* Everyone listens to some extent, but do they really hear what is being said? Effective listening requires attention, intention, and retention. It is hard to be open to learning if you are hearing another melody. Mentees must be active listeners and learn to hear both what is said and what is unsaid. Can you leave behind the chatter in your own head and really focus on what someone else is saying?

7. *Follow-through.* You need to do what you say you will do and do it as promised. If you don't execute, it will eventually compromise the trust in a relationship and upend your learning progress. Follow-through includes being organized and a good time manager in order to meet commitments. What is your track record when it comes to delivering on your promises?

8. *Reflection.* Reflection, as stated before, is a significant tool for facilitating the growth and development of mentee, mentor, and the mentoring relationship. It is the springboard to action and further learning. Being comfortable with the process skill of reflection means being able to step back, evaluate, process, and consider the implications of one's own experience in informing future action. How good are you at stepping back and seeing the big picture?

9. *Initiative.* You are the driver in this relationship, which means stepping up to the plate and asking for what you need when you need it. Hoping that your mentor will tell you, lead you, and be directive is not productive in helping you sustain the learning. Are you comfortable in making the first move?

10. *Valuing differences.* One of the benefits of mentoring is the exposure to different perspectives. During the course of your relationship, you are likely to hear perspectives different from your own. There may be positional differences, generational differences, learning style differences, or gender or ethnic differences. Can you be open to those perspectives and ideas and welcome them?

Self-awareness about your skills is an important step in preparing for your mentoring relationship. Self-awareness about how you learn helps make your mentoring experience more productive. We turn now to a discussion of learning style.

KNOWING YOUR LEARNING STYLE

Learning style can have a dramatic impact on a mentoring relationship. It influences how you work with your mentoring partner. It will also help you discern what kinds of learning opportunities would work best for you. We focus on learning style because of the centrality of learning to the mentoring relationship. Knowing how you learn will not only help you in a mentoring relationship but it will also help you in other situations. For example, knowing your learning style can help you be more collaborative, solve problems more easily, build and maintain other relationships in your life, create more motivated, engaged, and productive teams, and make better decisions.

At Leadership Development Services, we are great fans of David Kolb's Learning Style model (http://www.haygroup.com/tl/Questionnaires_Workbooks/Kolb_Learning_Style_Inventory.aspx) and use it as a tool for mentoring preparation. Kolb's model focuses on four styles or ways people perceive and process information. To determine your predominate learning style think about your own learning experience and your personal strengths and challenges. Focus on how you learn now, not how you would like to learn or how you think you should be learning. Then review the following four descriptions and see whether you can recognize yourself in one of them. Keep in mind that all of us are a blend of the four learning styles and what you are looking for here is your preferred style, the one on which you rely the most when you learn.

Diverging Learners

Some people perceive information concretely and process it reflectively. They learn best by reflecting alone about what they are learning and then sharing ideas and feelings. This style, called *diverging,* describes individuals who like to explore possibilities—the more ideas the better. They enjoy brainstorming and have fertile imaginations. Visioning comes quite naturally to them. They are inclusive and place a high value on preserving harmony and consensus. Their creativity is exciting and energizing to those around them. The downside is that when too many ideas are presented at once they often become indecisive. In the name of harmony they are conflict-adverse and often forgo their personal opinions. For example:

> *Isabella was regarded by her coworkers a team player. Everyone counted on her to be there, to help and do whatever it took to get a job done. She always supported her coworkers' ideas during staff meetings to make sure everyone felt included. Everyone liked her fresh ideas and openness. Wanting to please her mentor and avoid creating tension during their meeting, Isabella avoided confronting her mentor when she really didn't agree with the goals and suggestions her mentor was making for her. Not wanting to ruffle any feathers, she called her friend afterward to complain about her feeling of being pushed in an unwanted direction.*

Assimilating Learners

Those with an *assimilating* learning style perceive information abstractly and process it by thinking things through in an integrated and rational way. Logic, order, and perfection are important to them. They have a talent for analyzing disparate facts and organizing them into coherent concepts, models, and theories. They are data-hungry and need trusted information and facts before they can make a good decision. And sometimes that decision making is slow in coming because they are still assimilating data. Such learners value procedures and systematic plans because they provide a rational order to things. They might gravitate more toward the Personal Reflection Exercise (PRE) than the visioning aspect of preparation. They are often dependent on others to provide the impetus for action. They can become too theoretical and may be seen by some as being overly cautious and more concerned with theories and models than their practicality. Often they are perceived as overly critical and skeptical.

> Last week during their mentoring session, Carol's mentor asked her a provocative question, "If you weren't in your current job, what other route might you have chosen?" It caught Carol off guard. She immediately began to mull over the various options she might have considered. After three long minutes of thought and silence, she still hadn't spoken. Carol was trying to sort out the possibilities in her head and wanted to be sure about her answer. Questions like this were not easy to for her to answer and doing it on the fly only made her nervous.
>
> Her mentor tried another tactic and decided to give her some homework. He asked her to draft a plan of what career development might look for her this next year. Carol spent a lot of time thinking about what might make realistic and appropriate goals for her plan. It took her several weeks and multiple drafts. She finally came up with a detailed grid that itemized each goal, its key objectives, and detailed strategies for achieving it. She e-mailed her plan to her mentor with a note, "I am not sure that I have it right. Please excuse the typos, I am sending this from my Blackberry."

Converging Learners

Converging learners perceive information abstractly and process it actively and quickly into a concrete solution. Their strength is practical application, strategic thinking, and planning. These doers thrive on time lines and are quick to ask about the bottom line before they tackle a problem. Sometimes they act too quickly, without enough data, and make wrong decisions or errors. They rarely change their position once they have made up their minds. They are direct and to the point but often impatient and prefer to do things on their own to make sure the job gets done.

> *Phil identified a direction he wanted to go in and, at his boss's suggestion, found a mentor to help him get there. He was skeptical as first that someone else might be able to offer him assistance. Since Phil had a very clear idea about what he needed to do and how to go about doing it, he was willing to invest some time to see if it actually paid off with results. He was pleased to find that his mentor had great contacts and set up some immediate connections that he thought would speed up his career move. However, Phil was argumentative and blunt in mentoring meetings when he disagreed with his mentor. He never backed down once he took a stand and was pretty firmly convinced that he is right. This often created tension in the room.*

Accommodating Learners

The *accommodating* learner perceives information concretely and processes it actively. The result is that such learners are accommodating to people and adapt well to new situations. They are energizer bunnies in executing plans and tasks. They are creative problem solvers and risk takers, and they invite change and like visioning even more than the diverging learners. They learn by trial and error. However, they may get bogged down in trivialities and get behind schedule. They often get bored easily and appear scattered, disorganized, and sometimes pushy and impatient.

> *Charlie was excited about working collaboratively with his mentor, a senior VP of the company. He was hopeful that it would help him get recognition and ultimately the promotion he so badly wanted. He appreciated the opportunity to share his ideas with someone from the executive team about how the company could improve their image and relationship with the customer. Recently Charlie was asked to prepare an overview of his career path for the next five years and the key goals he needed to work on to achieve those goals for a mentoring session. As it turned out, Charlie hadn't prepared anything specific. He had a lot of ideas in his head and planned on "winging" it.*

Working with Your Own and Your Mentor's Learning Styles

Many conflicts between mentoring partners arise out of lack of understanding of differences in learning styles and not significant points of disagreement. The style with which you will probably have the potential

EXHIBIT 2.2

Selected Learning Style Descriptors

Accommodating	**Diverging**
• Energizing people	• Motivating the heart
• Visioning	• Being imaginative
• Motivating	• Understanding people
• Taking risks	• Recognizing problems
• Initiating	• Brainstorming
• Getting things done	• Being open-minded
• Being adaptable and practical	• Valuing harmony
Converging	**Assimilating**
• Exercising personal forcefulness	• Using principles and procedures
• Solving problems	• Planning
• Making decisions	• Creating models
• Reasoning deductively	• Defining problems
• Valuing efficiency and timeliness	• Developing theories
• Being practical	• Being logical
• Setting goals and timelines	• Deciding with data

for greatest conflict is the style that is in your diagonal quadrant. If you look at Exhibit 2.2 below you can identify your diagonal quadrant.

Accommodators and assimilators are in diagonal quadrants, as are diverging and converging learners. As you review the characteristics listed under each heading you can see how people with these styles might frustrate each other. The person with a diverging style wants to think about ideas and the person with a converging style wants to get it done. The assimilator is data driven and the accommodator is driven by instinct. Even if you and your mentor do not have a good style match, being aware that you have a different style can make the difference between shutting down in frustration and working through any conflicts.

For example, you might need to think about things for a long time to make a decision (diverging style) and your mentor may be someone who likes to move quickly and have agendas and time lines in place (converging style). Conversely, you may prefer to read as much information you can (diverging style) and your mentor may only want the bulleted version (converging style). By communicating about how you learn best you will be able to make steady progress and avoid some stumbling blocks in the learning process. Knowing your mentor's style will help you in your interactions with your mentor. So, for example, if your mentor wants plans and time lines and your style is more free-flowing and conversational, you know how to adjust your interaction. The bottom line? Know your style and let your mentoring partner know how you learn best. Be aware of your mentoring partner's style. Learn to adjust your style depending on who you are interacting with.

• • •

Preparation is essential to make the most of your relationship, and it begins with you. Knowing yourself comes through honest, intentional, and focused reflection. The preparation you've done so far is going to serve you in good stead. It will position you to understand yourself and share that understanding with your prospective mentoring partner. And speaking of mentoring partner, it is now time to take what you've learned in this chapter and use it to find the right match for you.

CHAPTER 3

FINDING AND GETTING TO KNOW YOUR MENTOR

IN CHAPTER TWO you considered what you needed from a mentor and the skills, strengths, and approaches to learning you will bring to the relationship. This means you completed the groundwork to help you become a strong partner in a mentoring relationship. Now it is time to take that learning forward and consider what kind of mentor you need, given your situation. Specifically in this chapter we look at how to identify, seek, and select a mentor; ensure that you and your mentor are a good fit; and establish a relationship with a mentor.

People find mentors in a number of ways. Some formal programs make mentoring matches for mentees. Many involve mentees in some aspect of making choices that lead up to the final match. Some, while providing support and resources, leave the mentee sole discretion in seeking and selecting his or her own mentoring partner, much like in an informal mentoring relationship. If you are in a mentoring program and have been assigned a mentor, you may feel that the section in this chapter on selecting a mentor is not relevant to your situation. I encourage you, however, to read through this section anyway, as there are insights about what makes for a good learning fit between mentoring partners that you may be able to put to use in your mentoring relationship.

CHOOSING A MENTOR: A CRITERIA-BASED DECISION-MAKING MODEL

We choose our mentors or they choose us. In either case, your decision to participate in mentoring needs to be deliberate and well thought out so that you can make the most of the opportunity. Mentor selection is critical to achieving successful outcomes. The natural tendency is to zero in on chemistry when meeting with prospective mentors. If the chemistry doesn't feel right the inclination is to go no further. Rather than rely on chemistry alone, I recommend using a *criteria-based* decision-making model. It can help you make good choices and avoid those that don't support your talent and capability or are not otherwise in your best interest. Even if there are better choices, it is easy to bias our selection toward those that set us up for easy success. Without some sound criteria, our decisions can be flawed, and neither you nor your mentor is truly well-served. Often, the result is disengagement, disappointment, and wasted time. Using a criteria-based selection model helps you clarify just what you need and suggests possibilities you probably never thought about before. It keeps the focus on end results, needs, and wants. And most important, it minimizes personal bias and low-level decision making.

Exhibit 3.1 outlines the eight steps in the Criteria-Based Decision-Making Model that you can apply to help you decide which mentor is right for you.

EXHIBIT 3.1

Criteria-Based Decision-Making Steps

Step 1. Identify your goal.	Consider why you want a mentor. Define what you hope to achieve as your end result.
Step 2. Create a list of criteria.	Identify the qualities you want in a mentor.
Step 3. Determine qualities that are "must haves." (Musts)	Select those requirements that are non-negotiable from your list.
Step 4. Rank the remaining criteria. (Wants)	Rank order the remaining criteria in order of importance to you.
Step 5. List possible options.	Brainstorm a list of possible mentors.
Step 6. Eliminate options that don't meet the "musts."	Evaluate each possible mentor against the "musts." If the candidate cannot fulfill them, do not consider him or her further.
Step 7. Rate each option against "wants."	Compare how well each of the remaining options stacks up against your "wants." Assign a numeric rating (e.g., 1–10) for each potential mentor to measure how well he or she measures up against each "want."
Step 8. Make the decision.	Tally the numeric score to identify which of the candidates best meets your desired end result based on the criteria you established.

GOING THROUGH THE STEPS

Next I take you through the steps of the model, providing both instructions and examples from the experience of Will, who used the model to help him make a good choice of mentor.

Step 1: Identify Your Goal

The first step is to stand back and consider why you want to find a mentor. Having a mentor because it is the "in" thing to do is not a good reason. There is a greater purpose involved: articulate what you are seeking to learn and why it is important to you. In doing so you are building on the work you did in Chapter Two, in which you were asked to develop a personal vision and to reflect on past experiences and on previous supportive or mentoring relationships. After doing the exercises from Chapter Two you should have a better sense of what you want to achieve in the long term, information that will help you understand what you need in a mentor. It is important also to take stock of your current situation. Let's look at Will's experience of Step 1.

Will is an account executive on a sales team. He is relatively new in the business and anxious to learn. He has already shown enthusiasm, energy, and willingness to work hard. Among his peers there is a lot of competition, and very few people are willing to help him develop his skills and take an interest in his career. His boss recruited him with the promise that mentoring and coaching would be available. Unfortunately, two weeks after Will took the job, his boss was promoted and the company hadn't found someone locally to replace him. Will has decided that he needs a mentor to help guide him, develop his skills as a sales team member, and show him how to succeed in the company.

Step 2: Create a List of Criteria

Identify qualities you need in a mentor. Look at your current situation, but also reflect on your vision for the future and on what kind of support has worked for you in the past. This means building on much of the work you did in Chapter Two. To see this step in action, let's check in again on Will.

Will's current situation, since he was new to the organization, clearly indicated that he needed a mentor who was experienced and knowledgeable about this particular company. This may seem like an obvious quality that anyone might want in a mentor, but not necessarily. For many people, especially those who have experience with a company but are interested in making other changes, company-specific knowledge and experience may not be important qualities for a mentor.

When Will reflected on times that he had received truly helpful support, he remembered one person in particular who stood out. She was his supervisor on his first sales job. He had a great rapport with her from the start—they both liked joking around and he soon felt comfortable being honest with her about his ambitions. He also remembered that her door was always open, and he never felt awkward seeking her out. He realized that he needed someone who was both accessible and with whom he felt compatible. Finally, Will considered his vision for his future, which was eventually to oversee a large sales force, and he knew he needed someone who would understand and help him pursue his ambitions.

Here is the list of qualities Will developed:

- Experienced in sales
- Accessible
- Successful track record
- Knowledgeable about the field
- Compatible personality
- Committed to mentoring
- Go-getter style
- Shared interests

Step 3: Determine Qualities That Are "Musts"

Select from your list those requirements that are nonnegotiable; these are your "musts." It is important that you keep the musts to a minimum. Two or three qualities should be sufficient. If you choose more, you may significantly limit your choices down the road and inadvertently overly influence the outcome of your decision. If you think you have more than three musts, convert one or two of them to strong "wants."

When Will went through this step he came up with the following two items: (1) experienced in sales and (2) successful track record.

Step 4: Rank the Remaining Criteria ("Wants") in Order of Importance and Assign a Value to Each

First, order the criteria, putting the most important first. Then give each a value by assigning a number according to just how important it is. For example, Will assigned a value of 8 to both "committed to mentoring" and "go-getter style," which effectively gave them the same importance. He gave "shared interests" a 5 to reflect just how much lower it was in importance than those he rated as 8. You will use these values later when you measure your mentor choices against the criteria.

Here are Will's wants, ranked in order of importance:

1. Accessible (value: 10)

2. Compatible personality (value: 9)

3. Committed to mentoring (value: 8)

4. Go-getter style (value: 8)

5. Shared interests (value: 5)

6. Knowledgeable about the field (value: 4)

Step 5: List the Possible Options

In contrast to Step 3, here you will want to make sure that you do not limit your choices prematurely. In later steps you will be evaluating how the people on your list measure up against your criteria. If you don't have a roster readily available, use your networks to cast a wider net by getting referrals from both inside and outside your organization. For Will, this step was relatively easy because he had a wide pool of potential candidates from which to draw. He came up with four good possibilities:

1. Daniel, the new regional sales manager. Daniel has been warm and friendly to Will, but since he moved offices he has been swamped. He now comes to Will's office once a month for two days to work with the team.

2. Emilio, the senior account executive in the office. Emilio is a very successful sales rep, and has bragged that he will get Daniel's job because he is the top performer, and he probably will get the appointment. He has been friendly to Will but not very helpful.

3. Ana, senior sales representative who works for one of Will's suppliers in town. Ana and Will hit it off immediately when they had to work together to solve a customer problem. She is a good listener and was very helpful to Will in dealing with the problems they faced. Her calm, assertive style helped resolve the dispute.

4. Steve, a professor of Will's from college who taught sales and marketing. Steve had a lot of experience before becoming an academician. Will enjoyed his classes and learned a lot from him.

Step 6: Eliminate Options That Don't Meet the "Musts"

This can be a very powerful step. It may be frustrating to simply eliminate a number of people right away, but if you have correctly identified the qualities that your mentor must have, do not confuse your decision making by continuing to consider mentors who really can't provide what you need. In Will's case, his two musts—"experienced in sales" and "successful track record"—made him realize immediately that he probably needed to eliminate his professor, Steve, from the mix because Steve didn't meet the criteria of a successful track record. Will crossed him off the list.

Step 7: Rate Each Option Against "Wants"

You will be using a scale of 1–10 to rate how each potential mentor stands in relation to your wants. Let's look at the process Will went through to rate Emilo.

1. Accessible—Emilio was rated high because his desk was right next door. Will gave him a 9.

2. Compatible personality—Emilio didn't fare well here; Will was turned off by his cocky attitude. He got a 4.

3. Committed to mentoring—Will had to guess here, but everything he sensed about Emilio was that he was not a mentoring type of guy. He gave him only a 3.

4. Go-getter style—Will had to admit that Emilio was strong in this department. He gave him a 10.

5. Shared interests—Here, too, Will really didn't know Emilio well enough to comment so he neutralized the grade, giving him a 5.

6. Knowledgeable about the field—Emilio was strong here and scored well with a 10.

Will continued to complete the evaluation of each mentor, trying to fairly evaluate their strengths and weaknesses. The final results are shown in Exhibit 3.2. Notice that the rating each candidate received for a criterion is multiplied by the value assigned that attribute. For example, Emilio's rating of 10 for being "knowledgeable about the field" is multiplied by 4, the value that Will had assigned that attribute. Doing this allows you to factor in the relative importance of an attribute to the score each candidate will receive.

Step 8: Make the Decision

To make your decision, do the math and total each column. If you have been diligent and honest with yourself, you will have a numeric evaluation of the candidates that indicates who best serves your well-defined musts and wants. Each candidate will have an accurate rating, and the final total will pinpoint the most appropriate choice for you. This model will also allow you to move down the rankings if your first choice proves unavailable.

EXHIBIT 3.2

Using the Criteria-Based Decision-Making Model to Select a Mentor

Decision Goal: Choose a mentor who will help me be successful in sales		Option #1	Option #2	Option #3	Option #4
		Daniel	Emilio	Ana	Steve
Musts					
Experienced in sales		Yes	Yes	Yes	Yes
Successful track record		Yes	Yes	Yes	No
Wants	**Assigned Value**				
1. Accessible	10	3×10=30	9×10=90	8×10=80	×
2. Compatible personality	9	9×9=81	4×9=36	10×9=90	×
3. Committed to mentoring	8	9×8=72	3×8=24	8×8=64	×
4. Go-getter style	8	10×8=80	10×8=80	7×8=56	×
5. Shared interests	5	8×5=40	5×5=25	8×5=40	×
6. Knowledgeable about the field	4	10×4=40	10×4=40	6×4=24	×
		343	295	354	

FINAL RECOMMENDATION: Select Ana as my mentor

Will was pleased with the results. Ana's high score was a strong indicator that she had all the right qualities to function as a good mentor for Will, which confirmed his gut feeling. The model allowed him to share this analysis and comparison with others to defend why he was looking outside the company for mentoring. The process gave him confidence that choosing Ana was a wise decision. He was, however, surprised that Emilio scored as highly as he did. This made Will realize that Emilio may have more to offer than Will had been willing to admit and that he needed to be more open to learning from Emilio, even if he wasn't going to ask him to be his formal mentor.

TALKING WITH POTENTIAL MENTORS

The criteria-based decision making model is a tool for identifying a mentor, but the tool for actually recruiting a mentor is *you*. Even when you have been assigned a mentor and you don't have to do the work of actively recruiting someone, your initial conversation is important. The criteria you developed and their order of importance can inform your conversation and inquiry when you approach your mentor. Whatever your situation, you are essentially asking someone to make a big commitment of time and energy to guide you in your development. Katherine Klein, a professor of management at Wharton School of the University of Pennsylvania, observes in Wharton's online journal Knowledge@Wharton, "Once a mentor sees that you're eager, the more likely it is the mentor will want to spend the time and social capital on you, introduce you to the right people, and so on" (reprinted in MentorNet News, 2008).

An article entitled "Why Mentoring Matters in a Hypercompetitive World" in *Harvard Business Review* says it another way, "If you want a mentor, start acting like you do and you will eventually find yourself connected with [people] who are invested in your personal development" (DeLong, Gabarro, and Lees, 2008, p. 121). When you are approaching a potential or assigned mentor for the first time it is important that he see that you

- Have genuine enthusiasm for your work
- Are conscientious
- Actively show interest in your future
- Are open to feedback
- Are committed to your own growth and development, curious, and ready to learn

Take few moments to review these bullet points and ask yourself two questions: (1) Would others see me this way? (2) How do I demonstrate

Recruitment Conversations

Scenario One

Eve, a quality supervisor in a mid-size manufacturing company, felt that without an engineering degree she was at a dead-end in her current position. She was interested in getting more into the operations side of the company, where she believed she could really influence quality and outcome. When she heard the new chief operating officer tell her own story at an operations review meeting, Eve realized this was the person she wanted to choose for her mentor. After the meeting Eve worked up her courage and asked her to lunch.

Eve: "Thanks for joining me for lunch. I really appreciate the time. Ever since the ops review meeting, I have been thinking about the story you told us about your career journey. It really struck a chord with me because it is my hope to one day be doing those very same kinds of things. I know that you are very busy. I am wondering, however, if you could find some time to meet with me on a regular basis for mentoring. I'd like to take advantage of the company mentoring program. I want find a similar path that would work for me, get to know more about the field and more about the opportunities and potential in it. I could learn a lot from hearing about your struggles—especially being a woman in this male-dominated field. I want to hear about what you did to overcome the obstacles that you faced because I really want to figure out where I can make my mark. I have given a lot of thought to where my strengths and weaknesses are and I'm interested in exploring what I can do to make changes. Maybe we could decide on a schedule that works for you, meet once a month, and talk or e-mail in between. I've checked it out with my manager and he would support the time. What do you think?"

Scenario Two

Kevin, a CPA by profession and a long-standing volunteer in a local nonprofit, found himself having been talked into chairing a capital campaign even though he had never done it before. He decided he needed to look for a mentor who had the skills and experience he lacked. After contacting a number of nonprofits who had used professional fund raisers in their campaigns, Kevin was given the name of a professional fund raising consultant. He used the referral as an entrée to make the telephone call.

Kevin: "I volunteered for an assignment in a nonprofit organization and now I have been recruited to be the head of their major fundraising division. I just don't feel like I have the skills to do this job even though everyone is saying 'you can do it, you can do it.' I have to lead a group of sixty volunteers; I have a budget—which I have never managed before. I've got to lead this fund-raising effort—be responsible for bringing in a million dollars in the next twelve months—and I don't know what the heck I am doing. I know I could go to the previous campaign chair but I simply can't relate to the style of the people who have done this before. First of all, they have all been here a long time, have a lot of contacts, and were able to raise money from their friends. That is clearly not going to work for me. I need your help. I need a mentor. So I think, on one level, I am asking you to hold my hand but on another level, I need real guidance. I feel like I could really learn something from you."

Scenario Three

Carmen was struggling in her current role as an HR specialist in a small regional sales organization where she felt isolated, insecure, and unsuccessful in influencing upper management. She was seeking a mentor who held a senior position in a similar organization and who had been able to successfully overcome the hurdles she now faced. She decided to seek mentoring help from a colleague from a larger organization who she saw periodically at HR conferences. After a presentation that they had both attended, Carmen asked her out for coffee.

Carmen: "It's been great seeing you at these HR conferences. At work, I never get to see anyone in our field. My company only has fifty employees and I do all the HR functions myself. This is a new job and I hope a new career for me. I had been a teacher for many years and entered this job to make a career change. I am eager to learn what I need to do to be my best and get to the next level. My long-term goal is to work in corporate HR, heading up training and employee development. I don't feel that what I am doing right now positions me well for that. But I have watched you at these meetings and I so admire your skills, background, and experience. You are doing what I hope to be doing in a few years. So I was wondering if we could get together occasionally. I'd like to pick your brain about what I am thinking and to see if I am heading in the right direction and get your ideas and feedback."

these attributes? For those of you whose first conversation with a mentor will be a recruitment conversation, you will find examples of ways to word your request in the examples on the next page.

MAKING YOUR FINAL CHOICE: SOME THINGS TO THINK ABOUT

After you have met with prospective mentors—or if you have a mentor assigned to you, after you have had an initial meeting—ask yourself two questions: Is this a good fit? Does this person have the time, willingness, and sincere interest in mentoring me?

If you've been assigned a mentor, you may feel that you have no choice, but you do. If you suspect there may not be a good learning fit, speak up. The more preparation you have done, the greater your ability to understand whether someone is or isn't a good fit and to advocate for a change if necessary. Does your prospective mentor truly fit the criteria you set forth? If you are reasonably certain that he does, then you can launch into the serious work of preparing your relationship. But before you make a final choice, let me offer some caveats about what to avoid:

Supervisors as Mentors

To some extent, all supervisors engage in mentoring their employees. Usually this looks and feels like a series of mentoring moments or minutes and happens informally as part of their job. However, when it comes to a structured and formal relationship, there are some important things you should consider before you jump into a mentoring relationship with a supervisor. Being mentored by an immediate supervisor is a slippery slope and often limits the authenticity of the relationship. The relationship doesn't invite candor because an uneven playing field exists and risk taking is often compromised. Mentoring tends to focus more on day-to-day work issues and less on big-picture development issues.

Choices Based on Convenience

Avoid the trap of making the "easy ask" or selecting a mentor simply because she is conveniently located or you already have a relationship. If you have truly followed through on using the criteria-based model, you should be able to avoid this pitfall. Unfortunately, I have seen too many people talk themselves into a choice based on convenience (or allowed themselves to be assigned a mentor based on convenience) only to regret the choice later on because it wasn't a good fit.

Personality and Charisma

It is easy to get drawn into a relationship because someone is very charismatic and has an engaging personality. Look beneath the surface and consider your criteria or you may end up passing up an incredible learning experience with someone who is very wise and talented.

Now that you've found your mentor, it is time to get started on building the relationship. This begins by getting to know the person behind the criteria and letting her get to know you.

PREPARING THE RELATIONSHIP

If you already know the person who is mentoring you it is tempting to just jump into the business of mentoring and skip the process of preparing the relationship. Although you may be tempted, it is not a good idea. Mentoring signifies the beginning of a new kind of relationship and you need to start at ground-zero with a really robust conversation that focuses solely on this relationship as a mentoring relationship. No matter how many mentoring relationships you have had, each is a new partnership and therefore building trust in that relationship is the first order of business. One way to build trust is to come to your relationship prepared. The exercises you have completed up to now have contributed to your readiness for this conversation. Once your mentor has said yes, or your mentor has been assigned, it is time to arrange for your first meeting.

Initial Mentoring Conversation: What to Talk About

The initial conversation is an exploratory one in which you and your mentoring partner learn about each other, establish points of connection, and lay the preliminary groundwork for working together. Topics that you will want to include to enrich that conversation are itemized in Exhibit 3.3, along with specific strategies and some guiding questions.

Let's take these items one by one.

Take Time to Get to Know Each Other

You need to bring yourself to the relationship fully and completely and be open and honest. Does that mean that your mentor needs to know everything that ever happened to you? Certainly not. Your mentor needs to understand who you are as a person; your challenges, hopes, and dreams; and your past experiences. It is your responsibility to bring your mentor up to speed.

You'll also want to get to know your mentor as a person. Review what you know already and make a list of what you want to know. You might

EXHIBIT 3.3

Initial Mentoring Conversation: Preparing the Relationship

To Do List	Strategies for Conversation	Questions to Ponder
1. Take time to get to know each other.	Obtain a copy of your mentoring partner's bio in advance of the conversation. If one is not available, create one through conversation.	What kind of information might you exchange to get to know each other better? What points of connection have you discovered in your conversation? What else do you want to learn about each other?
2. Talk about mentoring.	Share your previous mentoring experiences with your mentoring partner.	What did you like about your experiences that you each want to carry forward into this relationship?
3. Share your learning and development goals.	Describe your career vision, hopes and dreams, and articulate broad learning goals and the reasons why they are important.	Why do you want to engage in this relationship? What learning goals would align with your vision of the future?
4. Determine relationship needs and expectations.	Ask your mentoring partner what he or she wants, needs, and expects out of the relationship.	Are you clear about each other's wants, needs, and expectations for this mentoring relationship?
5. Candidly share your personal assumptions and limitations.	Ask your mentor about his or her assumptions and limitations. Discuss implications for your relationship.	What assumptions do you hold about each other and your relationship? What are you each willing and capable of contributing to the relationship? What limitations do you each bring to the relationship?
6. Discuss your personal styles.	Talk about your personal styles. You may have data from instruments such as EI, MBTI, DiSC, and LSI.	How might each other's styles affect the learning that goes on in the mentoring relationship?

Adapted from Losis J.; Zachary, *The Mentor's Guide: Facilitating Effective Learning Relationships*. San Francisco: Jossey-Bass, 2000, p. 91.

be curious about your mentor's career journey. For example, how did she begin her professional career, who was it that helped her along the way, and what were some of her challenges? The goal is to establish points of connection immediately that you can build on later in the relationship.

Talk About Mentoring

Share your personal stories about individuals who had a profound impact on your development and learning. You have previously prepared to discuss your own mentoring and learning experience by answering the four questions under the heading Insights from Experience in Chapter Two, and as a result you should be able to see more clearly what you appreciated about them, what worked for you, and what didn't. Invite your mentor to share his mentoring stories. Learn from his experience, then talk about what you each valued in your experiences and how you might bring that to bear in your mentoring partnership.

You may have been in a mentoring relationship that was disappointing. Share your story about that relationship and see whether you can identify what went wrong and why. Apply those lessons learned to your new relationship.

Share Your Learning and Development Goals

Here's another instance in which having done personal preparation pays off. Describe your career vision and what led you to that vision. Articulate your learning goals as best as you can. Broad goals will suffice; they don't need to be precise at this point. Some examples of broad goals are to learn what it takes to be a better realtor, balance work and family life, or improve communication or presentation skills.

Determine Relationship Needs and Expectations

Be honest about what you personally need in a relationship. Do you need a brain to pick? Another set of eyes? An ear to listen? A shoulder to lean on? Someone who can help you get your arms around a problem? Do you need a helping hand? A kick in the pants? Talk about what you personally need to help you be successful in this relationship.

An honest discussion about expectations for the relationship is also critical. This means explicitly asking your mentoring partner what she wants, needs, and expects out of the relationship and stating exactly what you want, need, and expect as well. Putting these on the table and discussing them is essential to arrive at consensus about what is realistic and what isn't. This ensures that both parties are satisfied with the relationship.

For example, if you have the expectation that a mentor should be a friend and confidant, you need to say so. It's better early on to know whether or not your mentor is comfortable with this. If you find out that she isn't comfortable, that doesn't mean you have to end the relationship. It does mean that you two can discuss this and determine how you can work together given that expectation.

Candidly Share Your Personal Assumptions and Your Limitations

Instead of focusing on the relationship as you did above, now you focus on *personal mentoring* assumptions, specifically the assumptions you hold about your role and the role of your mentor. Ask your mentor about his assumptions. Talk about similarities and differences, and consider how they might play out in your mentoring relationship. Talk about your personal limitations in the relationship and find out about those of your mentor.

Assumptions   One of the most important items in Exhibit 3.3 is the sharing of assumptions. Our assumptions determine how and what we perceive and are a result of our past experience. They become our truths, which we convert into actions. What makes this discussion so critical is that each person in a mentoring relationship carries truths about their role (their assumptions) and these guide their behavior. If mentoring partners don't share their assumptions with each other, they end up with miscommunication, and that, in turn, can upend a relationship.

Spend time with your mentoring partner talking about your assumptions about each of your roles. It may be easiest for you to share the list of assumptions that you completed earlier in your preparation and ask your mentor how they jibe with his expectations. Does it look like you are on the same page?

How does this play out? Marisa assumes that Howard, her mentor, will be a sounding board and help her get through her day-to-day challenges, provide just-in-time answers to her questions, introduce her to his network, and advocate for her when it comes time for promotion. Howard assumes that his role as a mentor is to be a guide. In that role he is to ask questions to help Marisa find her own answers, focus on the big picture, and support her in reaching her career development goals and learning how to access the right people. Unless Marisa and Howard talk openly and frankly about these assumptions, Marisa will be looking for quick fixes, expecting answers, and 24/7 access to her mentor.

Limitations Each of us has limitations; whether personal, time-related, work-related, or physical. It is important to be up-front about any limitation that may affect the mentoring relationship.

Discuss Your Personal Styles

In addition to your learning style (see Chapter Two), you've probably taken other personality inventories or emotional intelligence instruments. Information about the results will help your mentor know more about you. For example, Kim is a pretty easy-going person and takes things as they come. She is not a worrier and is very accepting. Mark might tell his mentor that he has taken the MBTI (Myers-Briggs) and that he is an ISTJ (one of sixteen Myers-Briggs personality types) and that pretty much is how he operates. He likes structure, is not into "touchy-feely," and likes to tie up loose ends and therefore prefers to work on one goal at a time.

If You've Been Assigned a Mentor

If you have been assigned a mentor, make it a point to establish rapport and really get to know the person behind the title before you jump full throttle into the relationship. At the same time you will want to share yourself, your story, and your context. A mentor needs to be able to walk in your shoes in order to support and challenge you appropriately so that you can work toward achieving your goals.

At this point, you have laid the groundwork for your mentoring relationship by meeting with your mentor, learning more about her, and talking about your hopes, dreams, and what you want to accomplish. You have discussed mutual expectations and explored some initial opportunities for learning. With the relationship preparation work completed, you are ready to take the next step: building a foundation for your mentoring relationship to grow and flourish. The next phase of the relationship requires some negotiating with your mentor to establish agreements.

CHAPTER 4

Establishing Agreements with Your Mentor

WHEN MENTEES PROACTIVELY establish agreements they are more likely to achieve their desired learning outcomes and experience greater satisfaction from their mentoring relationship. Whether you are engaged in informal mentoring or in a more formal mentoring relationship, establishing agreements up front will ensure that your learning and the relationship stay on track.

The process of establishing agreements requires its own conversation to clarify mutual expectations, accountability, and outcomes. The agreements made during these "negotiating conversations" become the guideposts for balancing learning and the relationship. With agreements in place, obstacles are less likely to derail you or the relationship. You are less likely to take things personally when stumbling blocks do get in the way of your learning, because you have a process in place to deal with them.

Establishing agreements will enrich and focus your mentoring experience. A mentor who isn't experienced but eager to help you may be grateful for the structure that this conversation provides.

In this chapter, the focus is on the process of establishing agreements—taking broadly stated goals from your initial mentoring conversation and refining them, putting processes in place to assure that the relationship stays on track, and creating a strategy and work plan to help you make the most of your relationship. Exhibit 4.1 lists each component of the negotiating conversation and the questions that need to be addressed for each in order to establish the agreements that will serve as a foundation for your work with your mentor. We will explore these more fully later in the chapter.

EXHIBIT 4.1

Establishing Agreements

Components	Questions Answered
Well-defined goals	What do I want to learn/accomplish as a result of this relationship?
Success criteria and measurement	How will we know if I am successful? What is our process for evaluating success?
Accountability assurances	How do we assure that we do what we say we are going to do?
Ground rules	What are the norms and guidelines we will follow in conducting the relationship? Who will be responsible for what?
Confidentiality safeguards	What do we need to do to protect the confidentiality of this relationship?
Boundaries and hot buttons	What are the not-to-exceed limits of this relationship? What hot buttons do you have that might present barriers and boundaries?
Protocols for addressing stumbling blocks	What stumbling blocks might we encounter? What process should we have in place to deal with them as they occur?
Consensual mentoring agreement	What do we need to include to ensure that this agreement works for us?
Mentoring work plan	What are the steps for achieving the goals? What are the learning opportunities?

Adapted from Lois J. Zachary, *The Mentor's Guide: Facilitating Effective Learning Relationships*. San Francisco: Jossey-Bass, 2000, p. 95.

SMART GOALS

Goal setting is probably the most challenging aspect of establishing agreements for both mentors and mentees. SMART goals frame and define the focus of the work to be done, eliminate ambiguity, provide a framework for gauging progress and measuring success, ground the learning, and set a context for mentoring. They harness and focus energy and invite action. One mentor we interviewed noted the importance of clarity regarding goals, "We were not really clear about the goals despite the fact that we had talked about it up front. We should have been more specific and concrete. Lack of it made our relationship a meandering process that was not as helpful as it could have been to each of us." If goals are left too broad, neither the mentor nor the mentee will be satisfied with the learning process, the learning outcome, or the mentoring relationship. For example, the goal of "being a more effective manager" makes it hard to focus the learning and determine what a successful outcome might be. If, on the other hand, goals are too narrow—such as completing performance reviews within two weeks—they may not challenge you. This incredibly important topic of goals requires more examination. We turn next to the difference between a SMART goal and a not-so-smart goal.

A SMART goal is Specific, Measurable, Action-oriented, Realistic, and Timely. If a goal isn't specific enough, you may find it hard to focus the learning; if not measurable, knowing whether you have accomplished it is difficult; if not action-oriented, it may not lead to visible, tangible results; if not realistic, it is difficult to accomplish and both partners may lose enthusiasm for the effort. And finally, if the goal isn't timely, you may have difficulty maintaining momentum.

The conversation that takes place between you and your mentor leading up to the formulation of your goals is a critical part of establishing a mentoring agreement. Formulating SMART goals is an iterative process that requires time and good conversation. It usually begins with discussion of a fairly broad statement of intent—as in your initial conversation described in the previous chapter—and moves from the general to the more specific and focused. Ideally, the questions your mentor will ask you will help you sharpen the focus of your goal and articulate it in written form. (If goal setting is not your mentor's strength, I would encourage you to share this information on SMART goals with your mentor to ensure that you are working together with the same approach.)

The following list represents some of the more typical "starter" goals we hear from mentees. (A *starter goal* is the goal a mentee first presents to a mentor before it develops into a mutually agreed upon SMART mentoring goal.) Although the items on this list meet some of the criteria of a SMART goal, none of them meet all five criteria and thus represent a starting point for conversation with your mentor.

- Managing office politics
- Working on work–life balance
- Advancing career development
- Promoting innovation
- Team building

- Managing up
- Moving beyond glass ceiling

"Managing office politics," while a laudable and desirable goal, is an example of a not-so-smart goal. It is too global and lacks specificity and measurability. Likewise, "advancing career development" meets none of the criteria, yet it is a worthy goal. It, too, begs for specificity in describing what it would mean if achieved.

Let's rework a few of these into SMART mentoring goals. A common goal that surfaces more and more these days is finding work–life balance. It is a very appropriate starter goal but lacks focus, measurement, and specifics. As a SMART goal, it might be articulated as, "Manage my time better so that I can be home for dinner with my family at least three nights during the week." Reworked in this format, it captures the components of SMART: it is specific, can be measured, and is action-oriented, realistic, and timely.

Let's look at another typical goal, "building a team." Framed this way, building a team is a good start. It requires you and your mentor to discuss the issue, intention, and problems that underlie your choice of this goal. But to launch the work to achieve this goal, the goal needs a SMART makeover. This goal might then look something like this: "Building a more cohesive, collaborative, and efficient team so that I can spend more time leading than managing." Although the goal as stated is not as specific and measurable as the previous one, it nevertheless implies an ability to compare before and after and identify a successful outcome.

Not all goals are appropriate mentoring goals. It is important to consider the context in which you are being mentored, as well as the experience and expertise of your mentor. For example, if you have a personal goal of writing a best-selling novel, using your mentor at work to achieve that goal would probably be inappropriate unless, of course, that person has a track record in publishing. There are some topics that are simply inappropriate for mentoring relationships. We delve into this further when we discuss setting boundaries in a mentoring relationship.

Goal Setting: An Iterative Process

It may take several meetings to turn a starter goal into a SMART mentoring goal and identify the criteria for success. We begin by eavesdropping on a goal-setting conversation between Joan, a management consultant, who is speaking to her mentor about her goals in general terms. Next we follow her progress as she and her mentor create SMART goals. Later we see how she identifies the specific criteria by which she will measure her success.

Joan initially stated her goal like this: "I've worked for a very long time on a large account and feel really good about the work that I've done because it is so vital to customer satisfaction. However, because the account is large and the client so high-profile, there are limited personal opportunities for me to actually get in front of the client and manage projects. It seems to me that the more senior consultants are the ones who get the visibility and recognition and they may be unintentionally standing in the way of my development. I'd really like to be out front on this account, in some way."

What followed was an extended series of conversations over several meetings in which her mentor posed lots of probing questions. Initially, they discussed Joan's hopes and dreams and why she was committed to this account. He challenged her on her statement that senior consultants were unintentionally standing in her way. He asked what led her to that conclusion. It was a frank and lively discussion in which he asked her to consider what she might be doing that allowed others to take over. After some soul searching and in-depth conversation Joan realized that she needed to work to increase her visibility in the company. She also had to acknowledge that she sometimes felt intimidated in the presence of the senior consultants and often didn't speak up as assertively as she should. She shared a few situations in which she had allowed herself to feel distracted and unnerved during important presentations.

Her mentor's questions helped her refine her thinking from the broad to the specific and to clarify what she really wanted to accomplish through mentoring.

The articulation of these goals served as a platform for even deeper conversation about which competencies, which accounts, and what kind of visibility would work for her. This process of exploration helped Joan formulate and prioritize her initial goals. She was ready to start turning these goals into SMART goals.

Turning Your Goals into SMART Mentoring Goals

SMART goals generally fall into two categories. The first type, "do" goals, are skill based and short-term; they integrate what you are learning and practicing. They are performance-based. For example, technical skills, mastering conflict management and communication skills are all "do" goals. Joan's goal of developing and managing accounts is an example of a "do" goal. The second type of goal, "be" goals, focus on longer-term development goals, expansion of the mentee's perspective, and the big picture. These are often amorphous and harder to articulate (for example, coping with change, empathy, patience, openness to feedback, resilience, tolerance for ambiguity). "Be" goals lead to leadership development, career development, personal development, and significant change.

Not all goals will fit neatly into this dichotomy, however. There are some goals that fit both types. For example, listening is really a skill, but the attitude of becoming more open and receptive is a quality about you and is therefore a "be" goal. Some have suggested that the "be" goals are hardest to accomplish because they make the biggest impact on development.

You may be asking yourself at this point, Which of these two kinds of goals do I want to focus on in a mentoring relationship? The answer is both. You will find that you need to develop some skills (that's the coaching part of mentoring) and to develop yourself. The former contributes to the latter. You might start with the latter and work back to the "do" goals as you talk with your mentor. If you do the preparation work of defining a SMART goal, it can help jump-start your relationship because your focus will be clear. Exhibit 4.2 is the initial draft of Joan's SMART goals. Exercise 4.1, which follows the exhibit, offers some tools to help you make a first draft of your own goals.

Now, turn to Exercise 4.2 to evaluate the "smartness" of your goals and refine your draft goals.

SUCCESS CRITERIA AND MEASUREMENT

Once you've decided on what your learning goals will be, your next conversation should focus on what those goals will look like when they are accomplished. Stephen Covey's famous catch phrase, "begin with the end in mind," is precisely what is called for here. Project yourself into the future when you and your mentoring partner are celebrating your success. What will you both agree on that you have accomplished? What will you be proudest of? What will you be able to do? How will you be different then from how you are now?

Answering these questions will help you define your criteria for success. Once you have identified the criteria, think about how you will measure your success, and create some milestones to assess your progress. Let's look again at Joan.

EXHIBIT 4.2

Joan's First Draft

Do	Be
Increase my visibility and expertise in client services	Raise my confidence level in working with senior management
Manage complex accounts	Increase influence
Improve my presentation skills	

EXERCISE 4.1

SMART Mentoring Goals Worksheet

Things to Think About
Specific
What is it I am trying to accomplish?
Measurable
In what ways can my success be measured?
Action-oriented
What results will I be able to see when my goals are accomplished?
What concrete things will I be able to do as a direct result of accomplishing these learning goals?
Realistic
Are my goals achievable?
Are there additional resources that need to be available in order to achieve my goals?
Timely
What is the time frame for accomplishing my learning goals?

Do	**Be**

EXERCISE 4.2

SMART Goal Checklist

When you have successfully articulated a SMART goal you should be able answer each of the questions below affirmatively. If you cannot, it means more work is required to articulate your SMART goal.	
Question	**Yes/No**
1. Is the goal clearly future oriented?	
2. Is the goal realistic?	
3. Will the goal be challenging for me? (That is, is it a stretch goal rather than a maintenance goal?)	
4. Will this goal require me to make a personal investment of time, energy, and effort?	
5. Will this goal contribute to my growth and development?	
6. Does this goal require constructive feedback and candid conversations?	
7. Is this goal achievable within the time frame of this relationship?	
8. Will I feel a sense of pride and satisfaction in accomplishing this goal?	
9. Will this goal produce tangible and measurable results?	
10. Is this goal in my best professional or personal interest?	

Joan and her mentor explored each goal, the strategies they would develop to tackle each one, and, particularly, how they would measure progress. They agreed that a clear way to measure the goal of increasing her visibility would be to identify the number of times she was able to speak in front of the senior team. Previously those opportunities had been limited to once a month. She and her mentor determined that if she was participating in or leading three presentations, that would be a sign of success. Improving her presentation skills was somewhat easier to gauge. They decided that Joan would ask a trusted colleague to work with her when she practiced her presentations and then to sit in on her formal presentation with the team. They agreed that getting feedback and working on areas of improvement should produce results over time.

The goal of raising her confidence was going to be harder to work on and to measure. Her mentor shared some of his thoughts about ways to determine success and the strategies to get there. Joan was eager to calm the butterflies in her stomach and she felt she could make a pretty accurate measurement of her comfort level. Confidence was something they would be working on and talking about over the course of their mentoring relationship.

Exercise 4.3 offers a tool for recording criteria for success, measurements, and milestones for each of your goals. Once you complete it you will want to agree on a time line to review your progress regularly with your mentoring partner.

ACCOUNTABILITY ASSURANCES

Mutual accountability plays a key role in helping mentoring partners make the most of a mentoring relationship. It begins with a candid and open conversation to create shared understanding, shared commitment to action, and working agreements about some of the "softer" issues in a mentoring relationship. In this section, we focus on four specific areas: ground rules, confidentiality, boundary setting, and hot buttons. Whether you are engaged in informal or formal mentoring relationships, having ground rules, safeguarding confidentiality, and honoring boundaries are important accountability assurances.

Ground Rules

Ground rules are the norms or rules of the road to which mentoring partners agree in order to manage expectations in a mentoring relationship. Without them you may end up spending more time managing the relationship than

EXERCISE 4.3

SMART Goals: Success Criteria, Measurements, and Milestones

Goal		
Criteria for Success	**Measurement**	**Milestone**

Goal		
Criteria for Success	**Measurement**	**Milestone**

Goal		
Criteria for Success	**Measurement**	**Milestone**

actually learning from your mentor. Ground rules will help you avoid the problems that Dave, one of the mentees we interviewed, had in his mentoring relationship with his mentor, Catherine. "You know, she was so smart and savvy about people. My only regret is that I didn't have more time with her. I could have avoided some of the people problems I did have by getting her advice and insights more often. We never actually agreed on how often we would meet. We never established a clear schedule or time line. I think if we had talked about how often formally and informally we would connect, I would have felt more comfortable dropping in during one of my crises. I was frantic, but I had just been in her office two weeks earlier, so I was worried about using too much of her time. I think now that if we had set up a more structured time to meet, and she would have also said, 'but, come by or contact me whenever you need something,' I would have avoided a few more disasters."

As you discuss ground rules, keep in mind that they should not restrict the relationship. Their purpose is to encourage and support accountability. Some of the more common mentoring ground rules include the following:

1. We will meet a minimum of once a month for an hour.

2. Our meetings begin and end on time.

3. I will be in charge of scheduling the meetings.

4. We will always have a meeting date on the calendar.

5. We will set an agenda for every meeting.

6. We will put interruptions aside.

7. We will manage our time well.

8. Each of us actively participates in the relationship.

9. Our communication is open, candid, and direct.

10. We will have a closure meeting no matter what direction our mentoring relationship takes.

Once you and your mentoring partner have decided on your ground rules, be sure to calendar some checkpoints to determine whether the ground rules are working for you and your mentor or are simply providing unnecessary obstacles.

Confidentiality

Confidentiality is a topic that is often omitted in mentoring conversations because it can be an uncomfortable or difficult subject to talk about. Although some individuals fear that such a discussion undermines trust, it actually lays a solid foundation for building it.

Tanya, a graduate student, was enthusiastically talking about her mentor, Julia, and how wonderful the year's experience had been for them. Laughing, she reported that her colleagues called her and Julia the "dream team" and she had to agree. It had been a completely enriching and growth experience for Tanya. When we asked her to identify what made it so successful she zeroed in on her initial confidentiality conversation just as the relationship was getting started. She described that Julia wanted to clarify issues regarding confidentiality right from the start. Tanya was appreciative. Tanya knew that Julia had four other students she was mentoring and she was worried about whether Julia might talk about her to the others. After their confidentiality conversation, Tanya came away relieved, knowing that Julia wasn't going to be sharing her struggles and problems with the other students or with her faculty advisor. In the conversation, Tanya and Julia had some different ideas about confidentiality, but they discussed them frankly and openly and were able to quickly come trust each other.

Then fast-forward a year. Tanya's formal mentoring relationship with Julia ended as the semester came to a close and Tanya was then assigned to Paula, a faculty member with whom she would be working for the next two years. Their first meeting couldn't have been more different from that with Julia. At the end of their meeting, when Tanya could see Paula was wrapping things up, she said, "Maybe we should talk about confidentiality." Paula replied, "OK, if you want." But Tanya could see that she really wasn't invested in the conversation and even as she nodded and said, "Sure, I agree," on each issue, she didn't show any genuine concern or interest. Knowing that Paula also was going to be mentoring four other students, Tanya felt herself immediately close down and become guarded. Even though they have been in a mentoring relationship for a full year, they never managed to develop a trusting relationship. Tanya believes they could have had one if they had been mutually committed to a conversation about confidentiality.

There are a number of ways to approach the discussion of confidentiality. For example, you might discuss what confidentiality means to you and ask your mentor the same question. Building on your responses, you might consider the types of confidentiality safeguards you would both want to put in place. If this approach doesn't feel comfortable you might use the checklist in Exercise 4.4 to begin the conversation about confidentiality. If you find, as Tanya did, that your mentor doesn't share your concern with confidentiality, it is important not to give up. Bring it up again at another meeting.

Because people have very different views of privacy, your concerns may not seem immediately important to your mentor. It is your job to push for clarity in confidentiality agreements.

Exercise 4.4 is a tool that you can use to begin a discussion about confidentiality with your mentor. You may find that all of the items work for you or none of them do. The tool itself will help focus your conversation.

Boundaries

A candid discussion about the boundaries of the mentoring relationship sustains the focus on learning, manages expectations, and ensures mutual accountability throughout the duration of the relationship. When boundaries are left undefined or personal hot buttons not discussed, they can eventually undermine the relationship by deflecting energy away from the learning focus of the relationship. Although you don't want boundaries to be so loose that they may be misinterpreted, you don't want them to be so rigid that they constrain the relationship.

Some of the instances in which boundary crossing becomes an issue include a mentor or mentee suspecting the other of a breach of ethics or honesty; inappropriate conversation, language, or familiarity; infringement of mentor's time.

Marietta had been hired as part of a corporate diversity initiative. Each new hire was assigned a mentor to help him or her acclimate successfully and understand the culture of the organization. Marietta's mentor was Jim. When Jim asked Marietta about what attracted her to the company, she told him that she had been a stay-at-home mom for the last five years, but she was recently separated from her husband and in the midst of filing for a divorce and knew she had to get back into the workforce. She told Jim that the separation from her husband had been difficult and that she anticipated an ugly proceeding. She expressed appreciation for landing a demanding job so she could focus on something more positive than what was happening at home.

After that first meeting, Jim realized that he was uncomfortable spending so much time talking about Marietta's personal problems. Jim and Marietta set up a time for their next mentoring meeting where they could explore some of the challenges Marietta anticipated, what she hoped to get out of the mentoring relationship, and the goals she needed to work on. At the end of that second meeting, after the two had established some clear goals, Jim suggested that they set some guidelines and boundaries to frame their conversations.

Jim told Marietta that he felt pretty confident that he could assist in her in achieving some of her work goals around developing her accounting

EXERCISE 4.4

Confidentiality Checklist

Instructions: After you and your mentor partner have each completed this checklist individually, come to consensus about which confidentiality protocols you want to adopt for your relationship.

Which of the following assumptions about confidentiality do you hold?	Yes	No	Not Sure
1. What we discuss stays between us for as long as we are engaged in our mentoring relationship.			
2. We can freely disclose what we talk about in our conversations with other people.			
3. After our mentoring relationship has ended, it is OK to talk about what we discussed or how we related.			
4. If there is a demonstrated need to know, we can appropriately disclose our conversations, impressions, etc.			
5. What we say between us stays there unless you give me specific permission to talk about it with others.			
6. Some issues will be kept confidential while others will not.			
7. It is OK to discuss how we relate to one another but not the content of our discussions.			
8. It is OK to talk about what we talk about as long as it is positive.			
Are there other assumptions I hold that should be added to this list?			

Adapted from Lois J. Zachary, *The Mentor's Guide: Facilitating Effective Learning Relationships.* San Francisco: Jossey-Bass, 2000.

skill, but he was definitely not on comfortable ground dealing with marital issues. He acknowledged that she was going through some difficult personal issues that might easily distract them if they became the focus of their conversations. He suggested that the company's employee assistance program might be a good resource if she needed support, and recommended that they leave her personal issues out of the mentoring conversations. Marietta agreed. In fact, she told him she appreciated him bringing it up early so she didn't jeopardize their relationship unwittingly.

Exercise 4.5 offers some questions to stimulate a frank and honest discussion about boundaries.

Despite best intentions, boundaries are sometimes crossed and the learning in the relationship is negatively affected. The best way to respond is to have a strategy in place to deal with boundary crossing if and when it occurs. Here are some potential strategies to consider when boundaries are crossed. First, let your mentoring partner know that a boundary has been crossed. Second, refer to the ground rules outlined in your mentoring agreement. Third, describe the behaviors that clearly demonstrate how the boundary was crossed. Fourth, request that the behaviors stop. If your mentoring partner acknowledges that boundaries have been crossed, let her know you appreciate the understanding. If boundaries go unacknowledged and continue to be crossed, ask your mentoring partner to stop crossing the line. Then insist that they be stopped. If that doesn't happen, bring the relationship to closure.

Hot Buttons

Andy was mentoring Suzanne for six months and really getting frustrated. Suzanne was anxious to have a forum for talking about her ideas, but every time Andy challenged her on her thinking, or suggested another course of action, she became defensive and shut down. Andy was beginning to see that she really wanted a one-way relationship—a place to get affirmation and confirmation of *her* thinking, not a place to explore the best approach or broaden her thinking. Suzanne had pushed Andy's buttons and he was losing interest in committing the time to the relationship.

Each of us has "hot buttons," things that irk us and make us react negatively to situations. Think about the hot buttons you have that might present barriers and boundaries to your relationship and share them openly with your mentoring partner. Ask you mentoring partner about his hot buttons. Hot buttons often include not showing up, being late, coming unprepared to meetings, multi-tasking, and lack of follow-through, to mention a few.

EXERCISE 4.5

Discussion Guide: Boundaries

What are examples of boundary issues that we might face in our mentoring relationship?
Are there any topics, issues, or discussions that are out of bounds?
What is our process if boundaries are crossed?
What strategies would help us prevent crossing boundaries?

The Mentee's Guide by Lois J. Zachary. Copyright © 2009 by John Wiley & Sons, Inc.

PROTOCOLS FOR ADDRESSING STUMBLING BLOCKS

All relationships, at one time or another, come up against stumbling blocks, even with accountability assurances in place. In my research I have found that most mentoring partnerships face five common stumbling blocks: failure to meet regularly, unfocused goals, untested assumptions, breach of confidentiality, and lack of communication. You owe it to yourself and your mentoring partner to have a full discussion about the "what-ifs" and what you will do if they become a reality. That is, what stumbling blocks might occur, and if they do what process will you use to address them?

There are questions you will want to discuss with your mentoring partner:

1. What are some of the stumbling blocks we've each experienced in previous relationships?

2. What potential stumbling blocks might we anticipate?

3. What other internal and external factors might negatively affect the relationship?

4. What would be an indication that we've hit a stumbling block? (Answer for each of the potential stumbling blocks anticipated.)

5. What process can we agree on to deal with the "what-ifs"?

MENTORING AGREEMENT

Until now we have been looking at the individual components of the negotiating conversation. When taken together these shared understandings become the basic framework of your mentoring agreement. They fit together like the pieces of a puzzle into a coherent whole and become the repository of your conversation notes. The form your mentoring agreement takes is not as important as its content. Your mentoring agreement could be as simple as organizing your notes, or you may decide to summarize your agreements in a memo of understanding. Some mentoring partners draft a mentoring partnership agreement. This will probably be the case if you are involved in a formal mentoring program. Whatever form you ultimately choose to use, it should be user friendly and work for both you and your mentoring partner.

This mentoring agreement template (Exhibit 4.3) may suggest other forms and formats. It is important to record your mutual agreements somewhere so that you can refer to them. Documenting your agreement together helps ensure that your relationship will be a partnership. The process of

EXHIBIT 4.3

Sample Mentoring Partnership Agreement

	We have agreed on the following goals and objectives as the focus of this relationship:	Our measures for successful accomplishment of each of these objectives will be:
1.		
2.		
3.		

TO ENSURE THAT OUR RELATIONSHIP IS A MUTUALLY REWARDING AND SATISFYING EXPERIENCE, WE AGREE TO:

1. Meet regularly.

Our specific schedule of contact is as follows:

2. Look for multiple opportunities and experiences to enhance the mentee's learning.

We have identified the following opportunities for learning (e.g., projects, task forces, client teams, conferences):

3. Maintain confidentiality of our relationship.

Confidentiality for us means . . .

4. Honor the ground rules we develop for the relationship.

Our ground rules are . . .

5. Provide regular feedback to each other and evaluate our progress.

We will do this by . . .

At least once during the course of the next year, and again at the conclusion of the mentoring cycle, we agree to review this agreement and evaluate our progress and our learning. If we choose to continue our mentoring partnership, we may elect to do so, as long as we have discussed and agreed to the basis for that continuation. Should we decide to conclude the relationship earlier than we anticipate, we agree to do so with appropriate closure.

Mentor	Date

Adapted from Lois J. Zachary, *The Mentor's Guide: Facilitating Effective Learning Relationships*. San Francisco: Jossey-Bass, 2000.

creating the agreement is as important as the agreement itself. It accelerates the trust-building process and creates shared accountability. It gives you something to go back to when you hit a hitch, glitch, or stumbling block.

MENTORING WORK PLAN

Michael Watkins, author of *The First 90 Days*, makes the point that the actions you take in your first ninety days on the job largely determine your success or failure. He says, "Failure to create momentum during the first few months virtually guarantees an uphill battle for the rest of your tenure in the job" (Watkins, 2003, xi). The same might be said of a mentoring relationship. Once your mentoring agreement is complete, it is time to roll up your sleeves and create the strategy for achieving your goals. Gordon and his mentor did just that.

Gordon sought out a mentor to help him in his new position as communications director of WEBMATE, a web development company that specializes in electronic services for nonprofit organizations. He had been handed the mandate of rebranding the organization's image, products, and services for their Gen-X clients and growing business opportunities with this group. WEBMATE serviced hundreds of clients in its portfolio that included organizations as varied as one that rescued pit bulls to another that promoted the practice of quilting. Gordon didn't know where to begin.

His mentor helped him focus. He asked him a pointed question: "Why did they hire you?" The bottom line, Gordon understood, was to increase business with a specific group of clients who currently were underrepresented at WEBMATE. Together, he and his mentor determined that Gordon should begin by identifying specific clients whose target audiences were predominantly Gen-X readers. They also agreed that he needed to create ways to increase communication with and for the nonprofit leaders of these organizations whose needs and methods were vastly different than the more traditional nonprofit clients of WEBMATE. Together they created the game plan in Exhibit 4.4 to help them focus their efforts.

A solid mentoring work plan becomes a road map for momentum. Exercise 4.6 showcases a form you might use to draft a mentoring work plan. Keep in mind that it is not the form or the format that matters but the substance of the work plan. You may want to complete a separate work plan for each of your goals and then when you are done put together a comprehensive overview of work plan that includes all of your goals.

EXHIBIT 4.4

Gordon's Mentoring Work Plan

Learning Goal	Measures of Success
To develop expertise in implementing communication and business development strategies with Gen-X nonprofit leaders and their organizations	• 25% increased revenue from Gen-X organization by year-end; • Development and implementation of a new webpage design for Gen-X newsletters; • Three new products and services that respond to Gen-X clients

Objectives	Steps to Completion	Learning Opportunities	Target Date
Create new designs, approaches, information, and resources that respond to the needs and "language" of Gen-X clients	Identify 10 clients that focus on the Gen-X audience Meet with clients for feedback and survey needs Evaluate 20–30 web sites that focus on Gen-Xers and identify success components Identify technology needs and requirements Create a new model for Gen-X branding	Online classes E-letters and newsletters Interviews with target clients and other leaders	Begin interviewing clients immediately Complete survey of sites by Dec 2009 Talk with professionals in the field between now and July

First Step: Identify ten clients that focus on Gen-X.

EXERCISE 4.6

Sample Mentoring Work Plan

Learning Goal		Measures of Success	

Objectives	Steps to Completion	Learning Opportunities	Target Date

First Step:

The Steps for Completing Your Work Plan

Enter your learning goal and itemize your criteria for successful completion of that goal (your measures of success). Lay out the objectives. Objectives must be specific and measurable with visible results. They describe how to achieve the goal. A goal might be "to position myself to get promoted." An objective would be "completing three new projects that would provide me exposure to the executives in the company."

Once your objectives are identified it is time to look at "steps to completion." These are the specific steps you need to take to meet your objectives. For example, in order to "complete new projects," what will you need to do? Attend a conference? Take on a special assignment? Shadow your mentor? Make presentations? You will want to factor your learning style into designing this part of the work plan. Don't settle for low-level learning opportunities. Give due thought to learning opportunities that will be most interesting and challenging to you. Consider human as well as material resources.

Set a target date for completion of each of your objectives. Setting a deadline will keep the momentum going. Although you may need to renegotiate the time frame, knowing that you have a target date gives you a milestone by which to evaluate your progress.

• • •

In this chapter we've covered the nuts and bolts of establishing agreements. The time it takes to establish these agreements varies depending on how well defined your goals are and how well you know the person who is mentoring you. Please don't be discouraged if takes you several conversations to establish your agreements. It is essential that you formulate SMART mentoring goals. Your mentor should be able to assist you in this process and help you make sure that you are clear about your own goals. In the process you will learn more about yourself, your motivations, and the possibilities that lay before you.

Before moving on to the next and longest phase of the mentoring relationship, doing the work, make sure that all of your bases are covered.

1. Are goals are well defined and clear?

2. Will you know what success looks like when you see it?

3. Have you and your mentoring partner talked about each of your responsibilities?

4. Have ground rules have been developed and agreed to by you and your mentor?

5. Are you in agreement about how often to connect and when and who should do the connecting?

6. Have your operating assumptions about confidentiality been well articulated?

7. Have you put accountabilities in place for yourself, your mentor, and the relationship?

8. Have you developed a realistic strategy for dealing with obstacles to the relationship?

9. Have you discussed how and when the relationship will be brought to closure?

10. Does the work plan excite and motivate you?

Bases covered? Great. The real work of the mentoring is about to begin. Chapter Five offers strategies that put you in the driver's seat and help you get the most out of your relationship.

CHAPTER 5

DOING THE WORK

NOW THAT AGREEMENTS have been established, it is time to go to work *on* and *in* your mentoring relationship. As you move into this phase you are probably wondering how it is going to evolve. Will you and your mentor be compatible? Will your mentor live up to your expectations? Will you live up to your mentor's expectations? Will you be able to keep your relationship on track? Will you be able to make the most of this opportunity?

This is the time in a mentoring relationship during which you execute the work of mentoring, strengthen your relationship, and make tangible progress toward your mentoring goals, guided by your established agreements. Whether you are in an informal mentoring relationship or a formal one, you will want to ensure that you work effectively with your mentor to achieve your learning goals and that you develop and maintain a good relationship with your mentor.

Mentoring unfolds in many different ways. Each and every mentoring relationship is unique because the individuals who come to it bring their own unique personalities and contexts. In a formal mentoring relationship there are two levels of accountability, those that are internal to the relationship and those that are external—based on organizational requirements. In an informal relationship the only accountabilities are those to which you and your mentoring partner agree.

While some relationships just seem to flow, others meander. What makes the difference? The simple answer is doing the work and working the relationship. You must be self-directed in your approach and remember that you are in the driver's seat. This phase requires you to play an active role in making sure that you use your time well, the learning stays focused, the relationship grows, and you address obstacles as they occur. Before I discuss each of these three areas—time, learning, and relationship—in detail, let's look at a story that illustrates what can happen if you don't pay attention to these things.

Don was a very willing and energetic mentee and was particularly pleased that he had been matched with Saul as his mentor. Saul was the firm's champion of the mentor program and in everyone's eyes, including Don's, *über*-supportive. They spent considerable time in the first two meetings just getting to know one another and were delighted to discover a mutual passion for golf. They talked broadly about Don's areas of interest, identifying some learning gaps he had as a new law associate, and sharing their mutual hopes about a mentoring relationship. Together, they identified two broad goals to work on. Don's first mentoring goal focused on how to better use his billable time and manage his ongoing projects more efficiently. His second goal focused on developing an expertise in real estate transactions. Initially, all went well.

Saul and Don set up their third meeting to begin to tackle the goals. Don opened the meeting by describing the weekend's golf round. The hour they had set aside quickly flew, and although Saul enjoyed the conversation, they hadn't made much progress on Don's billing issues. The next meeting started off in a similar vein and it was hard for Saul to get Don refocused. Saul was getting frustrated. Don seemed incapable or unwilling to stay focused on his professional development.

Effective mentoring relationships strive to balance the relationship and the learning and work on both simultaneously. The learning needs to be centered on achieving goals that mentor and mentee set collaboratively. Without a focus on concrete, important, developmental issues for the mentee and without the discipline to use time wisely, mentoring meetings can become social interactions that don't lead to progress or results.

GETTING THE MOST OUT OF YOUR MENTORING TIME

Time is a challenge for mentors, mentees, and their relationships. Whether related to work, personal demands, or life in general, it seems that these days we just can't get enough time. We end up carving up time for everything and in the process the quality of our time becomes hard to maintain.

Lack of time is one of the most frequently cited reasons for lack of mentoring success. "We couldn't find the time to meet regularly." "We are both busy people and we have a difficult time getting our schedules to mesh." "We set aside the time and then something always comes up and we end up rescheduling more than meeting." These comments or similar ones may resonate for you. Time is an issue that isn't going to go away. As a mentee, you need to be able to manage and take advantage of the time that you do have with your mentoring partner. You *and* your partner need to make a commitment to honor the time, use it well, and monitor it.

Early on, before your relationship began, you considered whether or not you would have the time for mentoring. You and your mentor discussed how you would spend your time and how much of it would be required as part of establishing agreements. Now you are in the mentoring phase when time issues become most pervasive. You may find that with all the other day-to-day challenges, taking time for mentoring becomes less of a priority. But sometimes lack of time is a perception rather than a reality. We often assume we don't have enough time when, in fact, we really do but simply make poor use of it.

How You Spend Your Time

Dealing with time concerns requires an ongoing awareness of how time is spent. It is up to you to manage your mentoring time and take responsibility for monitoring it. Here's a tool that can help you evaluate your mentoring time.

Draw a circle on a piece of paper. This circle represents your mentoring time pie, the time you spend with your mentor. Divide the circle into sections (much like slices of a pie) according to how you spend your time. For example, you might spend a "portion" of your time shadowing your mentor. Another portion of your time pie might be spent reflecting on practice. Perhaps another section would be on day-to-day problem solving. Another section might be on feedback, or catching up with one another. After you've completed your mentoring time pie, share it with your mentoring partner and get some feedback as to whether your perception matches his or her reality. Then with your mentor discuss the following questions: (1) What do we need to do more of? (2) What do we need to do less of?

Some Strategies for Spending Time Well

First, make mentoring prime time. Focus on mentoring totally and completely when you are with your mentoring partner. Be fully present. Your mentor is giving you the gift of his time and you need to do the same. Turn off the cell phone, the e-mail, and bring your full attention to your conversations (face-to-face or virtual). Avoid the temptation to multitask and eliminate interruptions.

Second, come to meetings prepared. Ultimately, you will spend less time if you effectively manage the time you do have. This means that you will need to find strategies for using your mentor's time constructively and maximizing your time together. Follow through, and keep a record or a journal of what you are learning. Partner with your mentor to prepare meeting agendas when you can. At the very least, have a clear idea about what you want to accomplish.

Third, stop if you are wasting time. Time becomes an issue when you can't find enough of it. Acknowledge the need to occasionally call a time-out when life becomes hectic or when you aren't using the time you have wisely. For example, you may find that your role at work is changing or that you are facing a deadline and you are too overloaded to focus on mentoring. Or perhaps the meetings aren't as productive as they could be because you need to take a time-out to process what you are learning.

Monitoring Your Meetings

In the establish agreements stage outlined in the previous chapter, you and your mentoring partner developed some accountability assurances. Exercise 5.1 presents an accountability tool that you can use again and again.

You and your mentor may agree to use this tool periodically to ensure that you are staying on track. But even if you haven't agreed to do so initially, you should feel free to introduce this tool to your mentor at any time during your mentoring relationship. This may prove especially helpful if you suspect that your meeting time could be better utilized and you are uncomfortable raising the issue with your mentor. This tool provides a neutral approach for addressing this concern, as well as for monitoring the relationship.

KEEPING THE FOCUS ON LEARNING

Your learning is the heart of your mentoring relationship. This is the reason you are working together. It needs to be kept front and center. Although a strong mentor can help you, the responsibility for keeping the focus on your learning lies with you. You need to (1) search for and making the most of learning opportunities, (2) help your mentor provide the right kind of challenge, vision, and support, and (3) along with your mentor, monitor your progress toward achieving your SMART goals.

Searching for Learning Opportunities

Earlier we touched on the importance of discussing learning style in your initial mentoring conversation and then again as part of developing your work plan. You may be someone who values discussion (diverging learner). Or perhaps your preferred style is getting facts, information, and data (assimilating learner). Or maybe your modus operandi may be to get the work done yourself as quickly as possible (converging learner). Or perhaps you need to figure things out for yourself (accommodating

EXERCISE 5.1

Mentoring Partnership Accountability Checklist

Rate Your Meetings Against the Criteria Below:	Never	Sometimes	Most of the Time	Always
We meet regularly.				
We do a good job of communicating schedule changes that may affect mentoring meetings.				
We notify one another if we cannot follow up or honor our commitments to each other.				
We eliminate outside influences and distractions when we meet.				
We check out our assumptions.				
Our communication is clear and misunderstandings are infrequent.				
We check in with each other to make sure that we stay on track with the learning goals.				
We provide feedback regularly and make sure it is two-way.				
Our meetings are relevant, focused, and meaningful.				
We acknowledge and address conflict when it occurs.				
We are conscientious about safeguarding confidentiality.				
TOTALS				

The Mentee's Guide by Lois J. Zachary. Copyright © 2009 by John Wiley & Sons, Inc.

learner). Although your learning style is a useful starting point, there is an old saying that is particularly apt here: "If you do what you always do, then you get what you always get." One thing you don't want to get in a mentoring relationship is the learning doldrums, that is, becoming a victim of "the same old same old." Mentoring is an opportunity to experiment with new and different modes of learning. Exercise 5.2 is tool that you can use whether you are in a formal or informal mentoring relationship to expand upon your initial list of learning opportunities. New opportunities are particularly useful to consider in this phase of the relationship because you and your mentoring partner presumably now know each other better, and that knowledge allows you to be creative and innovative.

Another approach to expanding your learning opportunities is the cascade approach. First brainstorm as many ideas as you can as fast as you can. Draw a line under the last opportunity. Ask yourself, what opportunities might Bill Gates suggest if he were your mentor? What would Walt Disney film if he were making a movie of your learning opportunity? Think about your favorite color—what activities does that suggest? The goal here is to challenge yourself to think outside the box and expand your horizons.

Journaling: A Learning Opportunity

Don't overlook the idea of journaling as a learning opportunity. Although the thought of keeping a learning journal might make you uncomfortable initially, it is one of the most powerful ways to promote learning. It forces systematic reflection, helps clarify thinking, stimulates new insights, assists you in remembering specific details and information, captures the richness of your learning as you go along, and becomes a record of your experience that you can refer to time and time again.

Some Journaling Tips

Keeping a journal is a practiced discipline and requires a commitment to action. Commitment requires that you accept journaling as a discipline that works.

1. As you write, keep in mind three words: head, heart, and action. Include factual material, reactions, feelings, goals, and tasks.

2. Write regularly, after each meeting and in between. Even if you are not a journal person by nature, write something down.

3. Schedule journal writing time. If you don't schedule it, it will get lost on the back burner.

4. Review your entries regularly. Doing so will help you monitor your progress.

EXERCISE 5.2

New Learning Opportunities

Instructions: In the spaces provided below, jot down ideas that come to mind as you think about the topic "possible learning opportunities."

Learning Opportunities	Within the Organization	Outside the Organization
Where can I get exposure to new learning?		
What can I do to reinforce what I am learning?		
How can I accelerate my learning?		

Use the approach that works best for you. You may have been a diary writer at one time. Or you may have kept a learning log at one point in your career. Some people find sentence stems helpful in getting them started.

Ira Progoff (1975) offers three sentence stems to stimulate reflection: *At first . . . and then . . . and now. . . . At first* I didn't know where to begin. *And then,* once I got into it I couldn't stop writing. *And now* I couldn't imagine a day without writing in my journal. A response to "what stands out for me" or "questions in my mind" is often enough to trigger some good reflective journal activity.

To help me focus mentoring reflections I've developed a set of questions that I use as a journal template. See the box for these questions and sample mentee responses to those questions. You may want to use these or develop a set of questions that is comfortable and works for you.

Journal Entry

1. The most important work we did today.

   Today, it was all important and I mean all! I was amazed at how much we (my mentor and I) accomplished. We spent some significant time debriefing on the school walk-through that we did last week. We talked about a methodology for getting feedback on my performance as a principal from my staff and teachers. We addressed those challenging work and family issues that have been plaguing me all year.

2. The most valuable lesson.

   I realized that I saw and heard things in the classrooms I'd never seen before, even though I've done my own walk-throughs many times before. I don't know if it was her (my mentor's) probing questions or the fact that I was walking someone else through the school or a combination of both but I see that I need to work at becoming a more astute observer and listener.

3. How will I apply what I've learned?

   I am going to check my assumptions at the door and be more open . . . whether in staff meetings or in future observations, and I am going to raise probing questions in my debrief with them.

4. What are the biggest challenges ahead for me?

   I've got to create a new curriculum task force and the teachers are . . . well let's say. . . . Less than enthusiastic. We've got a deadline and I truly don't know if we can meet it.

5. What questions still remain for me?

   Time. How am I ever going to find enough to do a thorough job at this? With my son moving back home after college and my elderly mom needing more and more of my attention. . . . I don't know but I do know I am going to have to figure it out.

Monitoring Your SMART Goals

Setting SMART goals is critical to achieving learning outcomes. At some point during this phase you may discover that your situation or needs change and the learning goals you agreed on earlier in the relationship are no longer relevant or timely. Going through the motions of working on goals that are no longer important or opportune is a waste of your time and your mentor's time.

You may have achieved your learning goals in a shorter time frame than anticipated. If this is the case, it is time to reexamine where you are and reformulate some new goals or bring the relationship to closure. You may have identified what you thought were SMART goals but found them to be daunting or unreachable when you began to work on them. In this instance, you will want to redefine or reframe them with your mentor. Achievement of a goal often raises new challenges and learning needs. It may mean reprioritizing or abandoning some of your original goals. Exercise 5.3 provides a worksheet and some guidelines for reviewing your goals.

GETTING THE SUPPORT, VISION, AND CHALLENGE YOU NEED

Your mentor provides support, challenges you to stretch, and offers a vision of the possibilities. It is in this way that a mentor facilitates your growth and development. One of the things that you can do to stir the pot is to let your mentor know what you need. Here I describe ways that a mentor can fulfill needs in these three areas. As you read through these examples, think about the *support* you need and that would be most helpful to you, the types of *challenges* that would be most meaningful to you, and what you need from your mentor to *envision* a path for your own development.

Support

There are numerous ways that mentors can provide support. By listening they can get to know and understand your interests, professional and educational background, and point of view (in other words, your context). A mentor can offer support simply by checking in with you between meetings to give you friendly reminders and help you stay on track. Perhaps you need help balancing your personal and professional responsibilities. Mentors also offer support by sharing their stories and making the relationship really special. These are just some forms of support that mentees we have worked with have found helpful.

EXERCISE 5.3

Goal Audit

Review Your Learning Goals

What specifically are you and your mentoring partner working on right now?
Are you making good progress toward achieving your SMART goals?
If no, are the goals still relevant?
If yes, what specific things do you need to do more of to achieve your goal?
What are your next steps?

Vision

Mentors are in a unique position to help you open your eyes to new possibilities by offering a vision of what is available to you now and in the future. In general, a good mentor can help you see the big picture without getting lost in day-to-day concerns and details that can blind you to the possibilities. She can familiarize you with what to expect in certain situations, help you see how you can work differently with various people or form new working relationships, and serve as a model for you to observe in action. You may find it useful, for example, to shadow your mentor for a day or in certain situations to see how she handles the challenges of her job.

Challenge

To get the most out of your mentoring it is important that you challenge yourself and that your mentor challenge you to stretch, do things you haven't done before, take risks, and explore new ways of working. Mentors also guide you through these challenges. For example, a mentor might set a task for you or create some alternative scenarios that might enhance your ability to advocate for yourself with your boss or with others, present your ideas more forcibly, confront colleagues when necessary, or navigate difficult conversations.

Being thoughtful about your needs and stating them with clarity will help accelerate your learning and allow you to play an active role in making sure that your needs are being met. Asking for what you need is as easy as saying, "What I am really looking for is some advice about how to approach my boss." "What I really need is a new way of thinking about this situation. I am in a rut." "What will happen if I follow this path?" It is essential that you learn to understand what you need and ask for it.

MAINTAINING A GOOD RELATIONSHIP WITH YOUR MENTOR

The mentoring relationship must be built on a foundation of trust. As I discuss in Chapter Four, issues of confidentiality must be addressed and revisited often, especially in environments where there can be perceived repercussions. Mentees can only truly benefit from the power of mentoring when they are willing to be vulnerable and open. They need to talk about their weaknesses and areas where they need help, not only about their strengths.

SMART Communication

Developing and maintaining a good relationship with your mentor requires effective communication. The frequency, content, and manner in which you and your mentor communicate will determine your success. Mentoring partners who allow large gaps of time to occur between meetings threaten the continuity of conversation and the momentum toward goal achievement. Make sure that appointments are kept and meetings are rescheduled instead of cancelled. Mentees sometimes feel uncomfortable when their mentor's calendar is strained or crises develop that preclude mentoring meetings. Be persistent in pushing for regular communication.

The manner in which you and your mentoring partner communicate is also a factor. SMART communication (Shared Meaning, Authenticity, Respect, and Trust), like SMART goals (Specific, Measurable, Action-oriented, Realistic, and Timely; see Chapter Four), will contribute to your effectiveness. By modeling SMART communication your behavior will help influence the positive nature of your relationship. Let's look at the building blocks to successful communication with your mentor.

Shared meaning Shared meaning suggests that the two partners truly understand what the other is saying and meaning. Words communicate only a small portion of true meaning. Voice intonation and body language are far more likely to influence deeper meaning. It is too easy to just listen to words and draw conclusions. Therefore, it is up to both mentor and mentee to clarify their understandings and clarify their assumptions to make sure they are valid.

What can you do? Paraphrase and ask for clarification when important issues are being discussed. Summarize your understanding at the end of a mentoring meeting. When you begin to assume your mentor is expressing a particular attitude or you interpret body language in a certain way, stop and verbalize your understanding. For example, "John, when I suggested that I wanted to work on conflict management as a goal instead of strategic planning, the look on your face made me think that you disagreed. Were you thinking that was a mistake?"

Authenticity Communication can become muddled, masked, stilted, half-said, or even insincere for many reasons. Especially mentees who are assigned senior management mentors often feel uncomfortable speaking their minds at the initial stages. For instance, it is difficult to have an authentic conversation about your relationship with your supervisor with a mentor who has a personal friendship or relationship with that supervisor. If you are considering a career move outside the company you may feel awkward revealing your dissatisfaction with the organization or talking about your interest in leaving. You may have experienced a confidentiality breach in a previous relationship and be wary about revealing additional personal information for fear that the same thing may reoccur.

What happens when the communication isn't authentic in a mentoring relationship? Distance grows between mentoring partners. Conversation becomes stilted. As a mentee, you can easily forget what you have said and haven't said in previous conversations. You communicate cautiously and the other party usually detects your lack of candor. Other statements, authentic or not, may be questioned as well.

What can you do? Share your concerns about the safety in the relationship. For example: "I know you are good friends with my boss, so I feel a bit uncomfortable bringing issues to you about my relationship with him. How should we deal with that?" If you are concerned about the safety of discussing a career move: "One of the issues I have been grappling with is whether this organization is the right place for me in five years. I know for the next year or two I have a future here. Is it going to be acceptable to talk about life after this company, or is that not something that fits into the mentoring program?" If confidentiality is or has been an issue and you are uncomfortable addressing it: "I know that one of the things I value in this mentoring relationship is the confidence that I can say something here and it won't come back to bite me or be shared elsewhere. And I hope you have the same feeling and that that is important to you as well."

Respect No matter what issues you and your mentor are working out, it is critical that each of you feels respected. Even if you are being mentored by a senior manager, there needs to be an inherent respect for each other's point of view and value as a person. Respect can easily be undermined when either party speaks or acts disrespectfully, even if in jest. For example, a mentor can easily and unintentionally "put down" a mentee's idea with sarcastic humor. Although the mentor intends it to be funny, it can be painful and leave you wondering about the undercurrent message when something such as "Well, that's a typical statement made by you Gen-Xers." is said or "Just don't say that to anyone who matters in this organization." or "Are you nuts?" Respect is a two-way street. As a mentee you must also maintain respect in your mentoring interactions. This is essential if you are to establish a trusting relationship.

What can you do? If you sense disrespect, even if expressed humorously, and it is getting in the way of the relationship, you need to address it. For example, "Last week, when we were talking about my time management issues, you said I was 'just a slacker.' I know you meant it to be funny, but

I have been thinking about that comment all week, and I wondered if that is what you really think I have been doing."

Trust The bedrock of communication in a mentoring relationship is mutual trust between mentoring partners. When trust is present, an assumption of good intention exists in whatever is communicated. Until trust is established, that intention may be assumed but can easily be undermined. Trust is something that takes time to develop and is tested regularly.

What can you do? Be authentic. Don't break confidences. Follow through with what you say you will do. And if you can't follow through, say so.

Feedback

Success in meeting your goals and getting the most out of your mentoring relationships depends on your ability to draw on the feedback you get from your mentor (and others) and to act on it effectively. It is also essential that you learn how to give feedback to your mentor. Honest, respectful, and straightforward exchange of feedback is the foundation of a good mentoring relationship. The following story reveals just how important feedback can be:

Feedback Story

"I am here today," said a senior account executive at a recent seminar, "because I got hard feedback from a mentor who was willing to give it to me, and I was finally willing to hear it." Avi shared these words with a group of mentors who were talking about providing feedback to their mentees. Many in the group shared how difficult it is to balance maintaining a good relationship with their mentee and at the same time holdup a mirror to the mentee to show them behaviors that are getting in their way.

Avi stood up to remind the mentors how important it is to be frank and candid. He reflected on his own experience as a mentee some ten years earlier. Avi described himself at the time. "I was young, cocky, talented, and I knew it. I knew I was going to get ahead and I knew I was in line for promotion. . . . In retrospect I think people were trying to tell me that my style was getting in the way. I just wasn't willing to hear it. I thought I was doing pretty damn good on my own. I can only imagine what it must have been like to work with me."

Avi laughed at himself, and the group joined in. Everyone in the room knew someone like Avi, a young upstart who didn't take direction, input, or feedback. Every opportunity for performance review was filled with defensiveness. It is difficult to manage the Avis of the world who, if they didn't have the talent to deliver great work, would have been fired long ago. It was too hard on other staff to have them around. Some of the Avis ended up working on projects alone, too talented to dismiss but too problematic to mix with other employees.

Avi made a plea to the mentors. "Don't give up on giving feedback. Sometimes you have to be really direct and frank, even if it isn't your style. I would not be the success I am today if my mentor hadn't sat me down, looked me in the eye, and told me what I was doing was not working. He said it, and I listened. And in retrospect, it made me realize that a lot of other people were trying to tell me it wasn't working, but I wasn't hearing it. Thank God I finally got it."

Your Comfort with Feedback

Giving and receiving feedback are skills that can be developed. We outline below ways to improve your skills in this area; however, it is important as you work to develop your skills that you be aware of your comfort level. In our workshops we do an exercise in which we ask people to line up according to their level of comfort in giving and receiving feedback. What we usually find is that people are more comfortable giving feedback than receiving it. That finding is understandable. Although in many areas of life it is better to give than to receive, in a mentoring relationship it is important to be able to do both. Each aspect is challenging in its own right. There is an art to giving feedback effectively. Receiving it requires openness and receptivity.

How comfortable are you in seeking, receiving, accepting, acting on, and giving feedback? Is your personal reaction to getting feedback affecting your attitude? Use the tips and strategies in Exhibit 5.1 to help you increase your confidence and competence in asking for, receiving, accepting, acting on, and giving feedback effectively.

Seek Feedback

Mentees accelerate their development and advance their mentoring relationship by being proactive and seeking feedback. Mentors welcome it when their mentees come to them and ask for feedback. Don't wait for feedback to come to you. Take the initiative. Make it a habit to ask for feedback regularly. The more specific and descriptive the request, the more specific and helpful the feedback you receive will be. You might say, for example, "I am struggling with how to get more balance in my life. It seems like my

EXHIBIT 5.1

Feedback Tips and Strategies

What You Can Do	Tips	Strategies
Seek feedback	Be proactive about getting feedback from your mentor.	Be specific and descriptive in asking for feedback. Make sure that what you are asking for is clear and understandable. Be sensitive to others' time.
Receive feedback	See feedback as a gift and an opportunity for improvement. Be receptive and keep an open mind. Avoid being defensive.	Be focused. Listen and really hear. Ask questions for clarification. Acknowledge the other person's point of view. Thank your mentor for the input.
Accept feedback	Think about the positive messages you heard. Reflect on the information that surprised you. Challenge your own thinking.	Take time to digest the feedback. Catch yourself being defensive. Look for ways in which the feedback will help with your self-development. Discuss your insights with your mentor.
Act on feedback	Focus on your goals and priorities. Check in with yourself periodically to determine how you are doing. Move forward.	Develop an action plan. Communicate your plan to your mentor. Continuously look for ways to integrate what you've learned from the feedback you received.
Give feedback	Direct feedback toward something that is changeable. Offer feedback when it is most timely and relevant.	Set a context. Be specific and descriptive. Be nonjudgmental. Be authentic. Be respectful of differences.

work has taken over my life. I budget my time carefully every day but it runs away from me as I get into my work. I get home exhausted and seem to have no time to chill out. How do you make it work so well? What suggestions do you have for me?" Or, "I just received some feedback from my supervisor and it just doesn't make any sense to me. I think she doesn't get me, who I am, and how I work. I am wondering what your take is on this and if I am totally off base. I'd appreciate your honest assessment of my leadership strengths and weaknesses." Make sure that what you are asking for is clear and understandable.

Receive Feedback

Receiving feedback is a challenge for many people. It requires not only listening but really hearing the message. It is risky because the perceptions others have of your behavior may not match your perception (witness Avi's feedback story above). The important thing to remember is that you don't have to agree with it. You need to be curious about the impact of your behavior and not defensive. Keep in mind that others often judge us on our behavior, not our intent. Even if you disagree, look for the kernel of truth. Verify what you've heard and then put the message into perspective. Don't take it personally. Feedback is not about your worth, but about your behavior.

Accept Feedback

Getting feedback from someone else affects people differently. Some people have strong reactions. When that happens it is difficult to accept. You may need to vent either with your mentor or a friend, or just let the information percolate before you react to it. Some people react with surprise and even when the feedback is positive go into denial or dismiss it. You may be energized by the feedback and can't wait to use and apply it. In any case, the goal is to learn from the information and use it to expand your thinking and improve. Be open and ready to listen. It's OK to respond honestly to what you've heard, but it is important to do so without becoming defensive. If you are surprised, say so. Ask questions so that you fully understand the feedback. Share your insights with your mentor. "Andy, I am taken aback. I never realized that I came across that way. I am glad you pointed that out. Can you tell me what else you've observed since we started down this path?"

Act on Feedback

Through the feedback process you've gained some insights about yourself. The next step is to take that knowledge and use it to take your development to the next level. Acting on feedback creates momentum. You start by focusing on your goals and priorities, setting some milestones, and targeting check-in dates. Keep your mentor apprised of your progress. "It took me a week or two but the feedback finally sank in and it does make some sense. I went to my peers and asked them for feedback and they completely agreed with what you said. I guess I knew that about myself down deep; now I am going to make addressing it my number one priority. I would be open to your suggestion as to next steps."

Give Feedback

Giving feedback to someone is an act of caring. It is not simply a matter of offering advice or constructive criticism. To be meaningful, it must be relevant, practical, timely, and specific. The way it is delivered affects how it is received, so it needs to be well framed. This means setting a context for the feedback and directing the feedback toward something that can be changed. "Marie, I really appreciated all the links and resources that you sent my way after our last mentoring meeting. I know you worked hard to put it together for me and I really appreciate it. I need to tell you that I have always been a slow reader, and it just takes me more time to go through resources that require lots of reading. I usually keep that info to myself but I felt I needed to tell you. I do much better with the crib notes and more succinct information."

We've addressed the importance of feedback and what you need to consider as a mentee when engaging in feedback conversations. Exhibit 5.2 presents some conversation tips and starters for your reference.

Creating the balance between working effectively and growing a solid relationship with your mentor is the real work of this phase. Both require your focus and attention. The emphasis is on the "you" because you need to be able to step up to the plate and ask for what you need in the relationship while at the same time be open to receiving the wisdom your mentor has to offer. An effective relationship takes work and steadfastness. It requires using time well, ensuring you get the most out of your meeting time, and being smart about your communication and monitoring progress on your goals. None of this can happen without a respect for and openness to the feedback process.

Chapter Six takes you to the natural end of this phase of your mentoring relationship: coming to closure. When you attend to closure in a good way, you enhance the impact of the mentoring relationship.

EXHIBIT 5.2

Tips for Mentees in Engaging in Feedback

What to Do	How to Do It	Examples
Early on provide feedback about what works for you.	Cite what helps you and what you don't respond well to. Offer concrete examples.	"Here's the kind of feedback I am looking for …" "What works for me is …"
Be aware of your communication style and how it meshes with that of your mentoring partner.	Share information about each other's learning style and discuss the implications for feedback.	"I am someone who needs to think about what is said before I respond." "I am more receptive when I receive a balance of positive and negative feedback."
Identify incidents and areas in which you are seeking help and ask for feedback on situations that you did/can do something about.	Tell your mentor what you did, how you did it. Describe your thinking process.	"How do you think I handled it?" "What would you have said if that had happened to you?"
When you talk from your perspective, remember that there might be another reality.	When seeking feedback, set a context and be descriptive, but not defensive, so that your mentor can understand the situation fully.	"Here's where I was coming from." "The way I saw it was …" "What I was trying to do was …"
Check out your understanding of what is being said.	Listen actively. Clarify and summarize.	"If I understand what you are saying …" "Do you mean …"
Use a tone of respect, especially if you see things differently.	Take care not to be defensive or attack your mentor's feedback or point of view.	"I appreciate that you are trying to give me another point of view …" "I am wondering why you think that approach wouldn't work …" "Can I ask you a question about that feedback?"
Avoid responding to feedback when you are angry, defensive, or need more time to process it.	Ask for time to get the information you need. Faking acceptance doesn't work.	"To be honest with you, I need to think about that a little more." "I think I was hoping for a bit more support from you."
Think about feedback as movement forward rather than interruption from the journey.	Continuously link progress and learning to the big picture and the journey and learning goals.	"I have been focusing on the goal of… and your feedback helps me see a pattern I have developed that is getting in the way."

Adapted from Lois J. Zachary, *The Mentor's Guide: Facilitating Effective Learning Relationships.* San Francisco: Jossey-Bass, 2000, p. 153.

CHAPTER 6

COMING TO CLOSURE WITH YOUR MENTOR

CLOSURE OFFERS ONE of the most profound learning experiences of a mentoring relationship. This is the mentoring phase in which you reflect on what you have learned during your mentoring relationship and position yourself to continue the momentum of your own developmental journey long after the relationship is over. It prepares you to leverage the knowledge you have gained and move forward.

Coming to closure also allows you to redefine the relationship and comfortably move on. It doesn't necessarily mean that the relationship ends, but it does signify that it is the end to this phase of the mentoring relationship. You may choose to move on by renegotiating your current mentoring relationship and working on additional goals or completing some of the goals that you hadn't achieved. You may decide to work with a different mentor or to pursue your further goals without a mentor. You may opt out of mentoring or, if you are in a formal mentoring program, the prescribed time for the mentoring to end is reached.

The important thing to keep in mind is that coming to closure does not simply signify an end. Fully embraced, it is a process that leads to further action. Good closure catapults you forward. Although an individual's need for and comfort with closure varies, closure is essential for growth. Whether closure is unanticipated or planned, its importance cannot be overemphasized. It is during this conversation, or series of conversations, that deep learning takes place, appreciation is articulated, and celebration occurs.

WHY CLOSURE IS OFTEN A CHALLENGE

The closure phase of the mentoring relationship is often overlooked or ignored. By the time you reach this phase you may be meeting less frequently, so the temptation is not to engage in closure but let the relationship fade out naturally rather than formally.

Some people avoid closure in any relationship, and this carries over into their mentoring relationships as well. Mentees often avoid closure if they have relied heavily on their mentor and are not sure what the next step might be without them. They have been supported and sustained and now are uneasy about moving forward without their mentor. Some are simply uncomfortable showing gratitude or expressing the emotion they feel. Some don't wish to appear too soft, particularly if their mentor is not the "warm, fuzzy" kind.

As a mentee, you may be expecting your mentor to take the lead and let you know when the time for closure arrives. You may worry that you will be perceived as presumptuous if you take the initiative and say that you are ready to move on. You may be worrying about offending your mentor or be concerned that your mentor may feel hurt. You may have become friends with your mentor and imperceptibly have drifted into a more informal personal relationship as you've gotten to know one another.

It is easy to become complacent about not having closure, but complacency has a cost: missed opportunity. Coming to closure is an integral part of the mentoring cycle. Without it you miss an opportunity to experience mentoring to its fullest and to make the most of your mentoring relationship.

WHAT YOU MISS WITHOUT CLOSURE

What are the opportunities that mentees and mentors forgo when they don't go through the process of closure? Here is an illustration:

Martha was a senior manager in sales, and Mia, two levels below in the quality department, had her eye on advancement in the company. Initially, when the two had been matched, Mia was intimidated by Martha's out-there personality and fast-paced style. Mia, quiet and more reflective, was surprised that the mentoring committee had put them together. It was hard for Mia not to feel overwhelmed by Martha's pace, energy, and quick action.

They had decided to meet monthly, face-to-face, with a mid-month check-in via e-mail, and Martha had invited Mia to drop in if she needed something more from her. Mia was reluctant to take up too much of Martha's time. She used the two prescribed occasions to work on her goals and move them forward.

Despite making some progress, Mia could feel Martha's impatience with her. Martha always seemed to want more from Mia. Even though Martha would acknowledge her progress and complement her on her achievement or results, somehow Mia could feel that something wasn't right. Maybe she wasn't fast enough, dynamic enough, bold enough for someone like Martha.

As the year progressed, Martha became involved in a big sales initiative, and Mia could see it was difficult for Martha to give Mia any of her time. She sensed they were both relieved that the year was coming to a close and the prescribed time for their mentoring relationship to end was approaching.

Mia wasn't sure how to handle the last meeting. Because it had been a difficult relationship she was tempted to simply thank Martha for her help and move on without any discussion or reflection. However, giving in to that temptation would have robbed both Mia and Martha of a chance to learn and grow from the relationship.

Instead of taking the easy way out, Mia summoned up her courage and sat down and faced Martha. "I want to thank you for the time you gave me this year," she started. "I appreciate that the company was willing to invest in me. But there were some things I regret and I wanted to talk about those for a moment. I feel kind of awkward about this conversation. I wasn't sure whether or not I wanted to have to bring these issues up. Then I went over my notes from the training, and it made me realized how important it is."

Mia was uncomfortable, and found it more reassuring to look at her notes. Martha was calm and listened. "You know," said Mia, "when we started, you invited me to call on you whenever I needed time, and I didn't, thinking I was already taking up your time. Then, it became hard to schedule even our monthly time. Well, I just gave up and waited for you to contact me."

Martha replied, "I am pretty sure that six months ago you wouldn't have been brave enough to have this conversation with me. I've seen you really step up to the plate and become much more assertive these last few months. And I am especially glad we are having the conversation we are now."

Mia laughed. "You're right. But you don't know how anxious I was coming here today. But, still, I did it." She continued, "I am wondering what you think about where I am and what part of my goals I should still stick with. Our mentoring is over, but I have a few things that I really need to work on. I was thinking of talking to the mentoring committee to help me find another mentor. What do you think?"

"I can understand where you are coming from and it sounds like a good plan," agreed Martha.

This conversation was clearly pivotal for Mia. Not only did she receive Martha's affirmation that she was indeed becoming more assertive, she was able to use the conversation to enlist Martha's help in identifying goals and finding a new mentor.

HOW TO PLAN FOR CLOSURE

How do you go about planning a meaningful closure experience? Ideally, planning for closure should take place while you are "doing the work," if not before. Ask your mentor what he would like to take away from the closure experience and talk about your hopes and expectations for closure. Discuss the following questions: What would we ideally like to see happen when our mentoring relationship comes to an end? How do we want to celebrate our success? What would make it meaningful? What might get in our way of coming to a positive closure experience? Once you've determined the outcomes you both want, talk about the process and planning.

When planning for closure with your mentor, it helps to revisit the ground rules you set when you were establishing your agreements. Hopefully one of your ground rules was an agreement to end on good terms. Many mentoring partners adopt the no-fault rule, meaning that there is no blaming if the partnership is not working or one person is uncomfortable. If you haven't talked about it before, talk with your mentoring partner as you approach the time to bring the relationship to closure. The bottom line is that if closure is to be a mutually satisfying and meaningful learning experience, mentoring partners must prepare and plan for it.

Right about now you might be thinking, "All this is well and good but what do I do if my mentoring partner isn't interested in meeting again to have closure or doesn't think we need closure?" In that instance, if a closure conversation is not to be had, don't give up. You've played an active role in this relationship from the beginning by asking for what you need, and you may find that *you* need at least some closure for yourself.

CLOSURE CONVERSATIONS

Each mentoring relationship is different, so closure conversations will vary depending on the needs and personalities of the mentor and mentee. However, to reap the full benefits, your closure conversations should contain four elements: what you've learned (coming to a learning conclusion), how you will apply what you've learned (integrating learning), celebration and appreciation, and redefining of the relationship. Your closure conversation can take place over the course of a number of meetings or in a single meeting.

Coming to a Learning Conclusion

A learning conclusion is a highly focused and reflective discussion centering on the specific learning you have taken away from the mentoring experience. Even if the relationship did not live up to your expectation the focus is still on the process, progress, and content of the learning. You will want to make the most of this opportunity and thoughtfully prepare for this discussion. I've listed a number of questions for you to answer as you reflect on your learning. Even if you do no more than answer these questions you will have brought some closure to the relationship for yourself and learned from the experience. Other ways to prepare include creating a time line of your work with your mentor, identifying milestones, and marking events to stimulate your thinking. Or if you've kept a journal, now would be a good time to go back and review it. Here are the questions (see also Exhibit 6.1):

1. Did I achieve my learning goals? If yes, what did I learn as a result?

   If no, what got in the way? In what ways might I have contributed to the lack of progress?

2. What was the most valuable thing my mentor taught me?

3. What specific insight, approach, or perspective did I gain?

4. What else do I still need to learn?

5. What did I learn about mentoring? About being a mentee?

6. What did I learn about myself as a person?

7. What has being in this relationship taught me about myself as a learner?

8. What would I do differently in my next mentoring relationship?

Let's look at how Maggie and Ernie handle their conversation about learning conclusions.

The stage is set. The time is right, and Maggie and Ernie are ready to discuss their learning. Maggie begins by saying how much she has learned this past year and how far she has come in her development. "I've gained so much from this relationship. I'm so much more self-aware and confident. My competence has grown in at least three areas and I'm much happier at work." Ernie agrees and lets her know that he has also observed her progress, specifically her interpersonal skills, her confidence, and her ability to balance short-term objectives with long-term goals.

Maggie reflects on their different styles: "I now realize that I should have seen our different learning styles as an opportunity for me to figure out how to work with others who are different rather than resist it." Ernie stops and thinks about his own learning and then says to Maggie, "Let me chime in here. I've been thinking about my own style since we had that long discussion about learning style back in January, and it has given me pause to think about things that I might have done differently. I was so involved in my project six months ago that I think I didn't give you enough time when you needed it and I really apologize for that." (It was interesting, she mused, that Ernie brought that up because the only time in the relationship when Maggie felt short-changed was when she was feeling very vulnerable six months ago.)

She thinks for a moment and then tells him, "Initially I think I really took it personally, but it also taught me that I need to fight for the time I need. Those insights made me see that I tend to take things too personally generally and that I ought to think about developing a thicker skin." Ernie notes that he was glad that she was aware of that and acknowledges that he used to take things personally too and had to work really hard to become more resilient.

Maggie talked more about things she had learned and what she is going to do differently in the future and asked Ernie what he thought her next steps should be. He turned the question back to her. After she responded he added some other areas for her to consider, such as developing strategic thinking skills and becoming more effective at strategy building and implementation. Maggie was puzzled at first by his response and then realized that her failure to see the big picture in their relationship was very much aligned with strategy. "It's the strategic stuff that trips me up. The day-to-day stuff piles up and often paralyzes my thinking. I remember something you said to me last January. It was about taking the long-view and letting go of some of my perfectionist tendencies. You've taught me that there is a difference between managing and leading and that includes thinking of myself as a leader."

Ernie commented, "That is a hard one but once you make strategy a habit and learn to execute on it, it will become part of you."

Their discussion was a rich and candid one. It left both of them feeling good about the relationship and proud of the work they had accomplished together. More than that, it helped reinforce Maggie's learning, giving her an opportunity to identify and reflect on what she had learned and providing a foundation for the next element of closure—integrating learning.

Integrating Learning

Discussion of the learning conclusion is an important part of the closure conversation, but good closure doesn't stop there. The lessons learned from mentoring beg to be used again and again. The closure conversation expands on the discussion by pushing you to consider how you are going to leverage your learning. That is, now that you've completed your learning goals, how are you going to integrate it into what you do every day?

We turn to Adam and Bert to illustrate the point. Bert, a small business entrepreneur, was completing his MBA at a state university on the East Coast. Adam was his faculty mentor and had been working with him for a couple of years. To Adam, it seemed as though Bert was always in a hurry, moving from one project to the next very quickly. At first Adam had been put off by Bert's brusque and impersonal manner, but as he got to know him, he grew to like him and appreciate his intelligence and insight.

Still, the relationship hit some stumbling blocks along the way because of Bert's lack of openness. The good news was that Bert became more aware of how his personal failings affected his dealings with people. He commented on this to Adam when they had their wrap-up session. "I learned it is not as much what you do, but who you are. When I interact with people now, I am not just thinking about what they can do for me. I have always been a driven, organized person, running ahead on my own path. I have learned to slow down and seek out others and find out where they are. I now draw more from the learning of others and not just try to impress them with what I know. I also seek feedback and realize that it is a constructive way to grow. So much of my awareness is a direct result of working with you, I have become more introspective and open to feedback. Before, I would hear the positive feedback, but never the negative. I forgot that there were things I really did need to work on."

The focus is on how you intend to apply what you've learned. What will you do as a result of what you've learned? Bert talked about how he would take his learning the next step, "I intend to use what I've learned to heal a difficult relationship with one of my team members and to improve my relationship with my customers. I will continue to work on becoming more objective, less judgmental, and more open. The 360 degree feedback process was an eye-opener for me, something I intend to continue to do myself and encourage my employees to do as well."

To realize the full impact of closure, the conversation needs to be expanded to include discussion of the action steps you need to take next. Your mentor can help you identify opportunities to apply the tools you've learned and take your learning to the next level.

Celebrating Success

Celebration is a fundamental part of concluding a mentoring relationship. It reinforces learning and signals the transition process that redefines the relationship. I invite you to look for meaningful ways to celebrate what you've accomplished.

I recall a conversation with someone I was mentoring. We were approaching the end of the relationship and were well aware that our year together was almost up. We said that we wanted to do something that would involve learning for both of us and that would relate to mentoring in some way. We wanted an opportunity to sit down in a comfortable setting and discuss our relationship in terms of milestones, insights, and development. My mentee also was very clear that she wanted to identify her next level development goals and discuss possible mentor candidates to help her achieve them. We talked about several things that we could do to make it celebratory, but we couldn't come up with anything. Of course, there was always "lunch," but we agreed to wait until we could find something that felt special enough. As luck would have it, a few weeks after this conversation she discovered that Marian Wright Edelman, founder of the Washington Research Project and Children's Defense Fund and author of *Lanterns: A Memoir of Mentor*s (2000), was speaking in Phoenix about her mentors and the influence they had in shaping her life. The focus of our mentorship had been around developing strategies to mentor young adolescent girls. Prior to this particular mentoring relationship the mentoring needs of adolescent girls was unfamiliar to me. My mentee's passion had piqued my interest and as a result I began to read more about the nuances and challenges involved in those relationships. When she me called to suggest that we attend Ms. Edelman's presentation, I was just as enthusiastic as she was. We agreed that it would be a fitting celebration and that afterward we would go somewhere to talk about what we had heard and how that related to the work we had been doing in the relationship.

It took us a while to come up with a satisfying and fitting way to celebrate, but we did. We didn't celebrate just to celebrate but tied it into what we were learning. It was a perfect conclusion for my learning as a mentor. We listened to the speaker and then held our conversation over lunch. We talked about Edelman's message and how her message fit with my mentee's work and with mine. And then we talked about what she had learned, how she was going to use it in her work as she moved forward, and our plan for staying in touch.

Saying thank you and celebrating in a meaningful way is often a challenge for even the most creative or articulate people. It isn't necessary, of course, to find a major event to attend together. What is important is to find a way to acknowledge the work you have done together that honors your relationship. Doing so doesn't have to take a lot of words, and the words need not be elaborate. What matters is that they are your words and they are authentic.

An excellent example is a letter that I received as a member of an advisory panel that was mentoring the owner of a small business. The mentoring relationship had been challenging and ended abruptly. As individual panel members we had hoped we had touched the business owner in some way but really weren't sure until we received her letter. Here's an excerpt of what she had to say:

> *From the start, your guidance and suggestions were enormously helpful and I took each one as an honor and did my best to follow them. When things came to a crisis point with my business, it was no different. Every time I spoke with any of you, I took away a valuable gem in the form of guidance and perspective. You also shared your network, introducing me to even more wise ones and exposing me to further skill and opportunity. I have been so blessed to receive your mentorship and continue to be amazed by the amount of time, the depth and quality of information and advice, and your commitment to my business and my personal development. I am so respectful and appreciative of each of you. I also learned so much just by witnessing how you all carried yourselves. I will seek opportunities to support others in ways similar to that which you have shown me. It has been a precious experience to be mentored by each of you. You believed in me. And that has been what has mattered most. (Reproduced with permission.)*

Her words touched each of us and made us feel that, when all was said and done, we had indeed made some impact in her life. I know it brought closure for me and the other mentors. It made us feel that all the time and effort was worthwhile. I imagine most mentors would feel the same way.

Sincere expression of your appreciation is one of the greatest gifts you can give a mentor. The expression of appreciation and gratitude benefits you as well. It helps you bring closure to a mentoring relationship and move on. Even if your mentor says to you, "you don't need to thank me," push back and insist on taking the time to celebrate. Don't get talked out of it.

Redefining the Relationship

Your relationship with your mentoring partner will be different once your mentoring relationship ends. You may decide to continue the relationship on an ad hoc basis. Be proactive and talk about these changes before they take place and then move on. Discuss how the relationship will change and whether it moves from professional to colleague, friend, or ceases to exist.

You may have become friends with your mentor as a result of your experience. What would that friendship look like without a formal mentoring relationship attached to it? Are there expectations that the mentoring would continue informally? Often mentoring partners become colleagues. What would that look like? Decide how or if you will maintain contact with your mentor. Will you stay connected to one another and, if so, what will that look like? If you decide to continue your relationship what will be different? What will be the same?

Shelley had a wonderful relationship with her mentor, Amanda. When the twelve-month program came to an end, Shelley knew that she was going to be re-assigned a new mentor in the second year of her master's program. Shelly and Amanda began to talk about closure and had several conversations about what their new relationship would look like. Amanda expressed concern about how their relationship might interfere with Shelley's bonding to a new mentor. On the other hand, they both acknowledged that they wanted to stay connected. Amanda invited Shelley to call occasionally and send e-mail updates on her progress in the program. But she did suggest that Shelley refrain from using her as a mentor as she moved forward. Shelley understood the necessity to cut formal mentoring ties but was relieved that they would be able to maintain the relationship she so highly valued.

Exhibit 6.1 summarizes the four core elements of the closure conversation and the questions to keep in mind as you hold your closure conversations with your mentor.

WHEN IT'S TIME FOR CLOSURE

If you are in a mentoring program, your organization may have predetermined the length of the relationship. Typically the length is defined in terms of a specified number of months or years. In an informal relationship, the length of your relationship *may* be dependent on the completion of a specific goal or a specific number of goals. If either is the case you have a milestone in place to signal closure.

Ideally you have been checking in with your mentoring partner all along and the time to come to closure is clear for you. If that is not true in your situation, be on the lookout for signals that the relationship may be ending. Check out your perceptions and assumptions when the first indications appear. What you think you see may be a reflection of your own

EXHIBIT 6.1

The Closure Conversation: Core Elements

Core Elements	Questions to Address
Coming to a learning conclusion: the specific learning derived from the mentoring experience	Did I achieve my learning goals?
	If yes, what did I learn as a result?
	If no, what got in the way?
	What was the most valuable thing my mentor taught me?
	What specific insight, approach, or perspective did I gain?
	What else do I need to learn?
	What did I learn about mentoring? About being a mentee?
	What did I learn about myself as a person?
	What has being in this relationship taught me about myself as a learner?
	What would I do differently in my next mentoring relationship?
Integrating learning: applying and integrating what you learned and taking it to the next level	How will you apply what you've learned?
	What will you do as a result of what you've learned?
	What specific action steps you will take?
Celebrating success: reinforcing learning and expressing appreciation	What are meaningful ways to celebrate what you've accomplished?
	How will you express your appreciation to your mentor?
Redefining the relationship: spelling out how your relationship will be different once this phase of the relationship ends	What happens after the mentoring relationship?
	Do you want to continue to be in contact? If so, on what basis?

anxiety, fear, or hope. Even if your mentor wants to end the relationship and you don't, you must honor her wishes. Gauge where you and your partner are in the accomplishment of goals and objectives. If you've met all the goals and objectives, it is time to celebrate and move on.

Ending a Relationship Prematurely

Even if the life cycle of the mentoring relationship has been established in advance, there are situations in which it may make sense to end the relationship prematurely. Some examples include relocation or redeployment, promotion to the same position as your mentor, pregnancy or illness that leads to a long absence, a new project or workload that precludes time for mentoring, or a promotion or new responsibility that prompts a change in goals for which the mentor lacks experience. It is easier to identify events like these than it is to sense that something isn't working in the relationship that suggests it may be time to come to closure. It is uncomfortable to end a relationship with a more senior person because of the fear of reprisal or career suicide. These relationships go through the motions of mentoring, but the energy and enthusiasm are missing. The following story illustrates this point:

For Guy, the tell-tale signs were there. He was dragging himself to mentoring meetings with his mentor James because he felt he had to. They kept talking about the same old things and Guy was finding his advice irrelevant. Clearly, the relationship was lacking and Guy even wondered how valuable it could possibly be for James. Guy was also getting increasingly impatient. The longer he stayed in the relationship the more time and opportunity he was losing in furthering his career.

Truth be told, he never really felt the kind of personal connection to James that his colleagues described in their mentoring relationships. Initially, he agreed to participate in mentoring because he knew that top talent were being recruited for the program and he wanted to be counted among them. James, a senior executive in his organization, had been assigned as his mentor. Even as early as their first mentoring meeting, Guy suspected that it might be a bad fit. James was two years away from retirement and in the process of turning over responsibilities. A lot of their meetings were taken up with James sharing war stories from his thirty years with the company.

Guy had been hopeful that the relationship would change over time, but after six months was beginning to consider trying to terminate it before the year was up. However, he was concerned that doing so might be a poor career move. But maintaining the charade of a relationship was becoming a chore and he wondered if it was worth it. How long could he afford to wait if he was to make the career move that would get him on the fast track? On the other hand, was it worth making waves in the organization by closing it out with James? Guy finally decided that the wise move for him was to end the relationship, given that it really wasn't adding value for him personally or professionally. He figured that now was a good time to step up and act like a leader and not become a victim of circumstance. Guy knew that if he wanted to be a rising star in the company, he had to take the risk.

At their next meeting, Guy broached the subject. "I realize during our time together that your experience and the areas that you are most passionate about are really not where I am headed right now. Listening to your stories has been extremely helpful to me. I now have a much better understanding of the company and its culture, but I have also come to realize that the area of the organization that I want to focus on and where I really need some guidance is not an area of expertise of yours. I think that puts both of us at a disadvantage. Given the limited time that has been allocated for mentoring, I believe I now need a mentor who is actively leading the part of the organization I want to move into. I am hoping that maybe you can help me find someone appropriate for the role. Is that something you would be comfortable doing?"

Guy was relieved to hear James express enthusiasm for assisting him. James told him he was only too glad to help him find the right mentor. Had Guy continued the pretense of engagement in this mentoring relationship, he would have lost valuable time and the opportunity to get the learning he needed at a critical time in his career.

Moving On

However you bring your current mentoring relationship to a close—whether you are moving to a new phase of continued work with your mentor, saying goodbye, or entering into a new mode as friends or colleagues—once the work of closure has been completed, it is time to move on. Sometimes it is easier said than done. If you had learned to rely on your mentor, you may feel like Linus without his blanket with nothing to hold onto. If your mentoring relationship continues it is not going to be the same going forward. Whether the relationship morphs into a different form or you continue with your current mentor, you are in a place different from where you began and moving on to new challenges and, you hope, new goals. You will be likely to find, however, that in many ways your mentor is with you. Long after the relationship is over, you may find yourself thinking, what would my mentor have said about this situation? What approach or advice would he have given me?

Even though you expressed your appreciation to your mentor, once you've moved on, you may be prompted to express it again as you hear your mentor's sage advice reverberate in your head. I've often thought that timing for saying thank you was a little bit off. We thank people politely when they give us a gift because it is social protocol. Maybe thanks should be given when we actually use and reap the benefit of that gift.

A friend and I were discussing how difficult it can sometimes feel when mentoring relationships come to an end. For mentors and mentees alike there can often be a huge void. It is tempting to fill this void quickly, but it is there to teach us a lesson. The separation caused by the relationship's absence is a gift, an opening for growth and regeneration. It is an invitation to wisdom.

We know that the best mentors are mentees themselves and continuously commit to their own growth and development in the role. Consider paying it forward and becoming a mentor as well as a mentee. In the final chapter we delve into how you can best transition into that role.

CHAPTER 7

Making the Transition from Mentee to Mentor

YOU NOW KNOW from first-hand experience the value of having a mentor in your life. But did you know that there are payoffs equally big for those who mentor? Mentors consistently report that they gain exposure to new and diverse perspectives from mentees that enlarge their thinking. They learn about operations, practices, issues, and people in other parts of the organization to which perhaps they would not otherwise have been exposed. When mentors have the opportunity to share their experience and wisdom and then see a mentee grow and develop into their potential, it is not only personally and professionally satisfying but also often a career highlight. Now it is time to think about building on the skills you learned as a mentee and applying them as you grow into and develop in your new role, the role of mentor. And as you do, you will find that skills you use will transcend the mentoring relationship and add to your competence in other areas of your life.

So let's get started. In this chapter I invite you to shift your focus and prepare to transition into the role of mentor. We'll look at the role of mentor, discuss how you can prepare for that role, and offer some advice for new mentors.

THE ROLE OF MENTOR

Even though the role of mentor is different from that of mentee, there are similarities. Being a mentor requires use of many of the same skills that you had to develop as a mentee. I'll identify four of the most important skills mentors must cultivate. The first one, reflection, is the platform on which the other three—facilitation, listening, and giving and receiving feedback—rest.

Reflection

Although people "do" mentoring all the time, effective mentors are not just doers, they are also be-ers. This powerful combination makes them reflective practitioners. *Reflective* practitioners are aware of and consistently test their own their frames of meaning, assumptions, feelings, perceptions, and worldviews as a prelude to action. Being reflective is a state of mind and is necessary to promote optimal learning in a mentoring relationship. As reflective practitioners, mentors raise mentees' levels of awareness about their frames of thought and how they make meaning translate into action. To promote higher-level thinking and practice for yourself and your mentee, you need to be critically reflective about what you think and do. To that end, reflection begins in the preparation for the mentor role. It is an essential component of the preparation.

You can begin by reflecting on your personal motivation to be a mentor with Exercise 7.1. This is an important exercise in that your motivation can negatively or positively affect the quality of the mentoring interaction. When you hold a deep understanding of why you are doing something, you end up being more committed to it and better able to use your time and energy.

Assuming that you are now on board, it is time to reflect on your previous mentoring relationships and see what you can learn from them. Mentees who are transitioning to the role of mentor find Exercise 7.2 useful in several ways. Completing it takes you back in time and encourages you to recall what it actually felt like being a mentee in a mentoring relationship. The process of reflecting on your performance is a reminder of the centrality of the role of mentee and how important it will be for you to create a climate that will help your mentee make the most of the relationship.

Facilitation

Artful facilitation is the key to promoting shared learning, reflective practice, and deeper insight for your mentee. Most mentors are eager to share what they've learned, and the temptation would probably be to teach it all and all at once. The challenge for you is to help your mentee grow and develop not so much by inviting them to adopt your newly found or accumulated wisdom as by the way you ask questions. It is these questions that will move your mentees to deeper places of insight and perspective.

Mastery of facilitation skills will help you engage your mentee by encouraging self-reflection and ownership. Skilled facilitators know that specific kinds of questions draw upon the unique thinking and learning style of different mentees. (See Chapter Two for information on learning styles.) When the right kind of question is asked, deeper learning occurs. Effective facilitators maintain flexibility and openness to learning. You may find that

EXERCISE 7.1

Mentoring Motivation Checklist

Instructions: Check all the reasons that becoming a mentor appeals to you. Seven or more checkmarks in the "yes" column indicates that you are probably ready to begin the work.

Reasons Mentoring Appeals to Me	Yes	No
1. I have specific knowledge that I want to pass on to others.		
2. I find that helping others learn is personally rewarding to me.		
3. I enjoy collaborative learning.		
4. I find that working with others who are different from me is energizing.		
5. I am always looking for new opportunities to further my own growth and development.		
6. I want to see this person succeed.		
7. I am seeking an opportunity to enhance my visibility, reputation, and contribution to my organization or community.		
8. I am committed to leadership succession.		
9. I need to meet a performance requirement at work or in my profession.		
10. I want to do the right thing.		
11. I want to pay it forward.		
12. I am interested in mentoring a particular person.		

EXERCISE 7.2

Reflection on Your Experience as a Mentee

Think about your journey as a mentee and your relationship with your mentor(s) to answer these questions.

How did you do? Give yourself a grade.
What could *you* have done differently or better?
Is there anything you wish you had said to your mentor that you didn't say?
What kept you from saying it?
What lesson or lessons are you taking forward with you as you transition to the role of mentor?

you do not agree with your mentee's point of view, but your willingness to respect a different perspective is critical to creating a safe and trusting learning relationship.

Listening

The one attribute that mentees say they value most in a mentor is that they are good listeners. Mentors who are good listeners listen for the noise and for the silence and use what they "hear" as teachable moments to encourage reflective thinking. For example, "I noticed that whenever we start talking about your finance manager you get quiet. I am wondering what that's about and if that is something we need to address."

Listening is hard work. Often we hear the words but not the melody. That is, we hear the words being said but do not always "get" what is really being communicated. How well we hear what is communicated may have to do with our intention to listen, our inability to concentrate, or our failure to listen actively for understanding. As a mentor you need to be able to listen reflectively so that you can hear the silences and observe nonverbal behaviors, as well as the content and context of what is being said. When you listen reflectively your mentee knows that you care.

Effective listeners balance talking and listening. They are aware of how much they talk and how much they listen. One way for you to monitor your balance is to try this exercise. Draw a line down a piece of paper; on the left make a header that says "talking" and on the right a header that says "listening." You can use this paper as a visual reminder during mentoring to maintain a good balance between talking and listening. Or, use it to keep track of how much talking and listening you do by discreetly making hash marks on each side to indicate when you begin to talk and when you begin to listen. After your mentoring meetings you can estimate the percentage of time you talked and percentage you listened. This will enable you to track over time the balance of listening and talking. The balance should improve once you increase your awareness.

Balancing talking and listening is a first and important step. The next step is to assess your effectiveness at listening. To that end, I invite you to complete the Listening Dynamics Profile in Exercise 7.3. Once you've rated yourself look at your total profile score and compare it with the Interpretation of Scores section of the exercise. Then go back and look at each of the four areas: intend to listen, concentrate, check for understanding, use memory aids. Identify the area in which you scored the lowest and pick and commit to one strategy within that area that you will work on over the next ninety days. Identify a date ninety days from now, mark your calendar, and on that date retake the Listening Dynamics Profile. Your score

EXERCISE 7.3

Listening Dynamics Profile

Please rate yourself on the following listening characteristics, which apply to interpersonal listening and to listening to a speaker. Check the number that best reflects your position on each scale below. The higher the number, the more the description on the left applies to you. The lower the number, the more the description on the right applies to you. Add your points for your total profile score when you have completed the profile.

INTEND TO LISTEN	5	4	3	2	1	
1. I usually intend to listen carefully when another person is speaking.						1. I rarely intend to listen carefully when another person is speaking.
2. I continue to intend to listen even if I am "turned off" by the speaker's delivery.						2. I lose my interest and intent quickly if I am "turned off" by the speaker's delivery.
3. I maintain direct eye contact when listening to a person.						3. I look away or avoid direct eye contact when listening to a person.
4. I do not interrupt when listening.						4. I tend to interrupt people.
CONCENTRATE						
5. I concentrate fully when listening.						5. I find it hard to concentrate, my mind wanders, and I am easily distracted.
6. I mentally summarize the main points of what I hear.						6. I do not mentally summarize or review the main points when listening.
7. I focus my attention on what a person is saying during interpersonal communication.						7. I think primarily of what I am going to say next when listening during interpersonal communication.
8. I listen for evidence in a speaker's comments.						8. I do not listen for evidence when listening to a speaker.
9. I anticipate what a speaker will say next.						9. I find it difficult to keep up with a speaker and rarely anticipate what a speaker will say next.
10. I control my emotions when listening.						10. I react or argue before I fully listen and understand.
11. I keep an open mind when listening.						11. I make immediate judgments and jump to conclusions when listening.
12. I do not allow certain words to immediately trigger my emotions.						12. I strongly and immediately react when I hear certain words.

CHECK FOR UNDERSTANDING	5	4	3	2	1	
13. I do not make assumptions after listening without checking them out with the speaker.						13. I frequently make assumptions after listening without checking them out with the speaker.
14. I communicate my understanding of what I heard a person express by putting it into my own words and checking that it is what the person meant.						14. I do not convey my understanding of what I heard a person say, to that person.
15. I communicate my understanding of the feelings I heard a person express, to the person.						15. I do not convey my understanding of the person's expressed feelings, to that person.
16. I listen in order to understand another person's perspective.						16. I do not listen to understand the other person's perspective.
17. I ask open-ended questions when listening.						17. I tend to remain silent if I have questions after listening.
USE MEMORY AIDS						
18. I use memory aids when listening.						18. I typically leave everything to memory when listening.
19. I listen primarily for main ideas rather than every fact.						19. I listen for every fact rather than main ideas.
20. I use note-taking skills when listening.						20. I rarely take notes when listening.
TOTALS						PROFILE SCORE =

Total Number of Points	Interpretation of Scores
90–100	Effective listener
80–90	Good listener
70–80	Average listener
60–70	Poor listener
60	Highly challenged listener
62–70	Where most people actually score the first time they take this assessment

Adapted with permission from the Listening Dynamics Profile © 1987 Frank DiSilvestro.

should have improved. When you take it the second time, repeat the process, but pick a different strategy this time. Mark your calendar, work on the strategy for ninety days, and retake the profile. Your new score should be even better.

Feedback

Mentees count on their mentors for honest and constructive feedback. They want feedback in order to know how they are doing, if they are moving in the right direction, if they are meeting your expectations, and if you are getting anything from of the relationship. It is essential that you create an expectation of regular feedback in your relationship so that you can deepen and enrich your mentoring conversations.

Feedback needs to be candid to be effective. Often in a mentor's desire to protect the relationship or the mentee's ego, the mentor filters feedback. This "shielded" feedback is inauthentic and not as helpful as it might otherwise be. Remember that shielded feedback doesn't raise the bar; it lowers it.

Think about the feedback you received as a mentee. I am sure that there were times you were hungry for it, and you didn't want it or were even afraid to hear it. By habitually building feedback into your mentoring conversations you reinforce its importance.

Asking for Feedback

As a mentor you can model asking for feedback by asking a general question such as, "How are we doing?" You can also model it by asking your mentee more specific questions, such as, "How is the relationship going for you? Is the learning process working for you? Are we moving too fast? Is it too slow? " Be sure to ask for feedback on your feedback.

Giving Feedback

You will want to give feedback to your mentee when it matters most: at the point of need. When you do, focus on learning and behavior change, not personality. Strive to maintain a two-way dialogue and engage your mentee in the feedback process. One approach is to continuously check for understanding. Above all, balance candor and compassion. Be honest, authentic, and genuinely sincere.

Receiving Feedback

Your mentee needs to acknowledge the validity of the feedback you are providing if meaningful change is to occur. Encourage your mentee to keep an open mind. This is easier said then done. As a mentor you'll need to do the same. Your mentee may tell you that the advice you gave her is wrong or that you don't understand her situation or what she is trying to convey to you. You will need to model how to receive feedback by keeping an open mind yourself and not being defensive when feedback is negative. You can do this by acknowledging her point of view and summarizing what it was that she said.

Accepting Feedback

Although feedback is important to help the mentee get to the next level, it can sometimes be difficult to hear. Some mentees (particularly diverging and assimilating learners; see Chapter Two) will need time to consider and process feedback before they are able to move forward with an action plan. You can facilitate your mentee's acceptance of feedback in the following ways:

- Suggest the mentee take some time to think about what she heard.
- Ask the mentee to tell you what she heard as a way of helping her process the feedback.
- Set a time for the two of you to reconvene to talk about the feedback.
- Ask the mentee to develop an action plan based on the feedback.

Acting on Feedback

Helping your mentee formulate an action plan based on your feedback creates momentum. Ask for her ideas of what she might do differently. Pose challenging questions to help her develop new ways of thinking or acting. Suggest ideas based on what has worked for others in overcoming similar problems. Identify a plan together and use it to track progress.

Exercise 7.4 is a tool to help you monitor your own effectiveness as a feedback provider.

Drawing on these four skills—reflection, facilitation, listening, and giving and receiving feedback—ensures that mentors can adequately fulfill two additional important aspects of the mentoring role: accountability and communication.

Accountability

Accountability drives successful delivery of performance expectations and results. Feedback encourages accountability in subtle and not-so-subtle ways. It fosters goal ownership and nurtures commitment. Without shared accountability it is nearly impossible for a mentee to create the positive energy necessary to attain learning and development goals. Feedback helps promote accountability by aligning expectations and giving input to ensure quality and timely results.

EXERCISE 7.4

Feedback Checklist for Mentors

Use the List Below to Give Yourself Feedback on Your Feedback Effectiveness	Yes	Strategies for Improvement
1. I pay attention to and build on my mentee's unique experiences.		
2. I encourage my mentee to reflect on past experience and use it as a learning opportunity.		
3. I allow enough time for my mentee to integrate and reflect on the feedback I give.		
4. I regularly check in with my mentee to confirm that the learning process is effective.		
5. My feedback focuses on behavior that the mentee can actually act on.		
6. I regularly check my understanding about what is said.		
7. I use a tone of respect in providing feedback.		
8. I am sensitive to my mentee's learning style when giving feedback.		
9. I avoid giving feedback when I lack adequate information or the timing is inappropriate.		
10. I encourage my mentee to welcome feedback and see its value in making progress.		

Communication

Lack of communication stalls mentoring dead in its tracks. When trust exists, communication is likely to be open and frequent, and mentoring partners can confront issues, thus quickly resolving conflict and deepening their relationship. When lines of communication are closed, mentees become hungry for connection. They make assumptions about why their mentors haven't been in touch with them and often end up feeling slighted, disaffected, suspicious, and distrustful. Second-guessing, stalling, questioning, and frequent false starts occur without good communication. Feedback becomes impossible and accountability an illusion. The dynamic interaction of reflection, facilitation, listening, and feedback with accountability and communication contributes to and sustains trust in a mentoring relationship.

ARE YOU READY TO MENTOR?

The process of mentoring effectively can be learned and, as with most skills, the more frequently the use the more the improvement. Still, before you make the decision to become a mentor it is useful to consider which of the attributes of a good mentor you currently have and what it might take to develop others. Without at least a number of these attributes to ground you in your development as a mentor, you may find that it is too difficult to fulfill the varied and challenging responsibilities that will be asked of you. These responsibilities include everything from managing time and problem solving to skillfully brokering relationships, coaching, and conflict management.

As a springboard for thinking about how ready you are to start mentoring, I would encourage you to take a look at Exercise 7.5 and review each of the attributes listed. Which ones do you possess? Which ones do you need to work on developing? Do an honest and clear-eyed appraisal of yourself. If most of these are a challenge for you, you might want to wait before diving into a role as a mentor. If, however, you find that many of these are strengths and, more important, that you are excited about taking up the challenge of developing other attributes, then exploring work as a mentor is probably right for you.

Becoming a Mentor

There are many different paths to becoming a mentor. There may be a formal program in your organization through which you can volunteer. Perhaps you may be approached by someone new to your organization for informal mentoring, or you may have observed individuals who seem to need

EXERCISE 7.5

Mentor Attributes

What are your strengths? What are your challenges?

Mentor Attributes	Strength	Challenge
1. Approachable		
2. Capable of honest self-examination		
3. Care about and respect others		
4. Committed to being an active mentoring partner		
5. Committed to self-development and self-improvement		
6. Emotionally intelligent		
7. Empathetic		
8. Feel secure about myself		
9. Follow up on ideas, suggestions		
10. Goal-oriented		
11. Innovative problem solver		
12. Not threatened by others' success		
13. Open to new ideas		
14. Positive role model		
15. Reflective		
16. Resourceful		
17. Strong interpersonal skills		
18. Trustworthy and willing to trust others		
19. Value difference		
20. Willing and able to spend the time		

help whom you can approach. Remember Kendra in Chapter One? She was approached by Sandra, who volunteered to mentor her when Sandra observed that she was floundering.

Let's look at each of these scenarios from the vantage point of your new role as a mentor.

A Prospective Mentee Approaches You

Say that someone approaches you and asks you to mentor her. How would you go about deciding if you should accept the invitation? There are many considerations. First and foremost, you need to consider your own readiness, availability, and willingness to mentor. Second, consider what this prospective mentee brings to the relationship. Does she have the "stuff" that makes a good mentee? Is she competent, committed, conscientious, and both open and ready to learn? Third, consider whether you have the particular skills and experience to help this person on her developmental journey. Is there a *learning fit* between what she wants and needs to learn and what you have to offer? Fourth, would you be comfortable working with her? Finally, determine whether you are sincerely interested and committed to helping this person at this time.

You Approach a Prospective Mentee

You may have your eye on someone who you thought could use a mentor— a superstar, a future leader in the organization, someone who clearly has huge but unrealized potential. If you are not in an organization, you may know someone you think you can help succeed. Don't be afraid to approach him and offer to mentor. You might say something like, "John, I've been watching you and I think I can help you become a better leader in this organization. I admire your energy and your laser focus. In fact, I've been down that path myself and if you are interested I'd be willing to make myself available to mentor you." Several caveats apply here. Make it comfortable for the person you approach to say no without guilt. If you are this person's supervisor, be aware that mentoring a direct report is a slippery slope fraught with challenges. For instance, although you may be mentoring this individual informally on a daily basis as a result of your position, these are usually just moments and conversations—very different from developing a true mentoring relationship. Another challenge is that if you choose to mentor a direct report, consider the ramifications of that choice. For example, almost always those who are not approached will feel slighted or jealous.

Your Mentee Has Been Selected for You

In a formal mentoring program there is usually a protocol for making mentoring matches. It may be that mentees have a free rein and can choose whomever they like, or that they are given some names of possible matches and asked to talk with those individuals and prioritize their choices. In some programs, all of this is done electronically; the prospective mentee goes shopping online for a mentor. Sometimes the match is made using an algorithm or by committee, and the mentee or the mentor is assigned a mentoring partner to contact. Even though you may not have selected your mentee, stay with and trust the process. Don't get distracted by overanalyzing the selection. Put your assumptions aside and approach the relationship as a learner yourself. Be as open with your mentee as you would want the mentee to be open with you. Be aware that your mentee may resent the match if you were not his or her choice. One approach is to acknowledge this and move forward, building the relationship one step at a time.

Revisiting the Mentoring Cycle

And so the mentoring cycle continues. As part of your personal preparation you will want to review to the various phases of the mentoring cycle as laid out in the preceding chapters of this book. Exhibit 7.1 presents a quick summary of those phases, along with some of the essential questions that those phases must address.

Advice to New Mentors

No matter how much you prepare on your own for the new role of mentor, some mistakes are inevitable. Indeed, making and correcting mistakes is the best way to learn. Still, some common traps can be avoided.

Look Before You Leap

Don't agree to participate in a formal mentoring program without really understanding the time and resources required. Be sure you understand the precise purposes of the program, what is expected from you, and the intended outcomes of the program before you say yes.

Make Sure You Are in the Loop

Stay tuned to what is going on in the organization and in your profession so that you are current and can help your mentee avoid missteps. The advice and resources you provide need to be relevant and timely in order to be meaningful.

EXHIBIT 7.1

Mentoring Cycle: Questions for Mentors

Mentoring Phase	Can You Answer the Following Questions?
Getting ready	Am I clear about my role? Am I the best person for the job? Is this particular relationship right for me? Do I have the time to do justice to this relationship?
Establishing agreements: Negotiating	What are the mentee's goals? What are our criteria for success? Is there mutual understanding of roles and responsibilities? What are the norms of the relationship? How often should we meet? How often should we connect? What are our operating assumptions about confidentiality? What are the boundaries and limits of this relationship? What is our work plan? How and when will the relationship be brought to closure?
Implementing and doing the work: Enabling	Have we established a regular pattern of conduct? How well are we communicating with one another? What kinds of development opportunities am I providing to support fulfillment of my mentee's goals? How can I improve the quality of the mentoring interaction? Are we continuing to work at maintaining the trust in this relationship? Am I providing thoughtful, candid, and constructive feedback? Is my mentee using the feedback to take action? Are there some lurking dangers or "undiscussables" in the mentoring relationship? What additional learning opportunities, resources, and venues should we add to enhance the learning experience? Are we taking time to reflect on our partnership regularly? Is the quality of our mentoring interaction satisfactory?
Integrating and moving forward: Coming to closure	Have we proactively established closure protocols? What are the signals that indicate now is time for closure? How are we going to acknowledge and celebrate accomplishments? What are the learning outcomes of this relationship? For me? For my mentee? How am I going to apply what I have learned from this relationship? In what way(s) can I help my mentee think about taking her learning to the next level? Where does the relationship go from here?

Be Patient

It can take a number of meetings to get the relationship moving in an authentic way. Building a trusting relationship takes time and attention. Trust begins with communication and respect. Remember that you and your mentee may be operating on different timetables because of different learning styles, cultural differences, or even a learning disability. As you may remember from your experience as a mentee, it can take time to work out the kinks in a relationship.

Plug In

Know how and when to use technology appropriately. If your mentee is online and "plugged in," you need to be. This may be an opportunity for reverse mentoring, and your mentee can help you learn the tricks of plugging in.

Don't Make Your Goals Your Mentee's Goals

Your mentee's goals are his, not yours. Because they were right for you doesn't mean they will be right for him. And he may have a different view of what that goal fully implemented means for him than you do at this point in your career. Your responsibility is to make sure his goals are on target, are SMART, and provide the right amount of challenge.

Keep Your Biases in Check

Listen for understanding about what your mentee's needs are. The biggest challenge is to keep your own experience and biases out of the picture. But when your bias is showing, acknowledge it.

Don't Be Judgmental

Being judgmental sidetracks you. Your mentee's problems are unique to her, even if her problem is one you have heard before from others. The danger is to think, "This is just so and so whining again." Your approach should be, "What is the issue today? How does it affect her goals, short or long term?"

MAKING THE TRANSITION

As you've worked your way through this chapter and prepared for your role as a mentor you've created a picture about the kind of mentor you want to become. I invite you now to actually envision it and picture yourself in the role. What is the vision you want to grow into? What is your personal development goal as a mentor? What do you need to get there? What is your action plan? These are questions you need to think about in order to propel your own growth and development in the role of mentor.

As you engage in mentoring, you bring our own cycle, your own time-table, your own history, your own individuality, and your own ways of doing things to each relationship. For learning to occur, you must understand who you are, what you bring, and what your mentoring partner(s) brings to the relationship. You must also understand the complexity of the mentoring relationship and the ebb and flow of the learning process. In sum, you must prepare yourself to meet the challenge so that your efforts can have profound, deep, and enduring impact. A mentoring partnership involves conscious choice and challenges each of us to think about what we might become and to remember Ralph Waldo Emerson's sage words, "What lies behind us and what lies before us are tiny matters compared to what lies within us."

DIGGING DEEPER: AN ANNOTATED LIST OF HELPFUL RESOURCES

LORY FISCHLER and I put our heads together to come up with a list of resources organized by the chapter titles in this book to help you increase your competency, confidence, and comfort level. We hope that you will continue to dig deeper and learn all you can about yourself and the practices that will help you make mentoring work for you.

Chapter 1: The Power and Process of Mentoring

Tuesdays with Morrie by Mitch Albom. (New York: Doubleday, 1997)

> Albom reconnects with his former mentor (a college professor) after many years. This time his mentoring relationship is qualitatively different from the earlier one. He is not the same person he was in college and is open to a different kind of learning. His mentor, too, is in a different time and place in his life. Whether you are a mentor or mentee, this heart-warming story has many lessons to teach about life and the dynamics of a mentoring relationship.

The Secret of the Seven Seeds by David Fischman. (San Francisco: Jossey-Bass, 2006)

> The story of Fischman's personal struggle as a stressed-out successful entrepreneur is told through the fictional character of Ignacio Rodriquez, who suffers a heart attack. A spiritual guide helps Ignacio heal and find his path in the secret of the seven seeds: self-knowledge, meditation, egolessness, service to others, goodness, balance, and freedom. Mentors, too, are guides that help us discover our path. This book contains many lessons about balance and the search for happiness.

Mentor: The Kid and the CEO by T. Pace and W. Jenkins. (Edmond, OK: MentorHope Publishing, 2007)

> This inspirational parable focuses on the significance of having a mentor in your life and the importance of being ready to be in the relationship. It will speak to you on many levels—from your own personal development to paying it forward. The words of wisdom at the bottom of each page are an added bonus and are representative of those a mentor might impart.

Chapter 2: Preparing Yourself to Make the Most of Mentoring

Now, Discover Your Strengths by M. Buckingham and D. O. Clifton. (New York: The Free Press, 2001)

> Self-awareness is an essential part of your preparation as a mentee. Instead of focusing just on your gaps and weaknesses, this book shows you how to identify your strengths so that you can improve them even more to become a better contributor to excellence and performance in your organization. You will find a code embedded in the cover of the book that you can use to go online and complete an instrument that will identify your "signature themes." Once you've completed the assessment you will want to dive back into the book and get the interpretations and strategies you can apply and work through with your mentor.

Communicating Your Vision by T. Cartwright and D. Baldwin. (Greensboro, N.C.: Center for Creative Leadership, 2006)

> Having a clear vision will help you decide what it is you really need to learn. This resource is a guide on how to take your vision to the next level. It provides the ABCs of visioning and addresses why a vision is essential. It also offers straightforward tools and examples that you can use to communicate your vision to your mentor.

Awakening the Leader Within by K. Cashman. (Hoboken, N.J.: John Wiley & Sons, 2003)

> The story of Bensen Quinn, a CEO, serves as a catalyst to begin to explore your own development, inside and outside your workplace. There are many valuable lessons that come to life as you read through the case studies, stories, and details of Bensen's journey. Each chapter concludes with a "Wake-Up Call" of reflective questions that will move your thinking to the next level.

Becoming a More Versatile Learner by M. Dalton. (Greensboro, N.C.: Center for Creative Leadership, 1998)

> Dalton's monograph is another practical and action-oriented guidebook from the Center for Creative Leadership. It will aid you in aligning your learning strategy and your learning goals. It suggests ways to go beyond your own traditional learning tactics and explore new options for learning and thinking outside the box.

Finding Your True North—A Personal Guide by B. George, A. McLean, and N. Craig. (San Francisco: Jossey-Bass, 2008)

> Based on the best selling book *True North,* this field guide/workbook offers a road map for helping leaders do the important work of defining their leadership, their passion and their authenticity. The exercises in this book are useful even if you are not in a leadership position. You can use them to take your conversations with your mentor about your life passions to a deeper level.

Self-Directed Learning: A Guide for Learners and Teachers by M. Knowles. (Chicago: Follet Publishing Company, 1975)

> We would be remiss if we didn't include this short classic reference for two reasons. First, learning is the purpose and process of mentoring. Second, self-directed learning (SDL) is the means by which learning takes place in a mentoring relationship. SDL involves identifying learning needs, formulating learning goals, using human and material resources (i.e., mentors), and evaluating your own learning. This book will guide you in developing your own competency as a self-directed learner so that you can make the most of your mentoring relationship.

The Kolb Learning Style Inventory (version 3.1) by D. A. Kolb. (Boston: Hay Group, Inc, 2005)

> This booklet contains the learning style instrument, an interpretation guide, background and application information for strengthening and developing learning style skills, working in teams, resolving conflict, communicating at home and at work, and considering a career. It also includes exercises for further exploration based on learning style.

Type Talk, The 16 Personality Types That Determine How We Live, Love, and Work by O. Kroeger and J. M. Thuesen. (New York: Tilden Press, 1988)

> Myers-Briggs Type Indicator (the MBTI) is a scientifically validated instrument, based on the work of Jung, for understanding ourselves, our

preferences, and how we perform and interact in a variety of settings. It is used in many ways by organizations to strengthen relationships and increase employee productivity. If both you and your mentor each have an understanding of your Myers-Briggs, you already have a tool for speaking the same language and building the relationship.

Let Your Life Speak: Listening for the Voice of Vocation by P. J. Palmer. (San Francisco: Jossey-Bass, 2000)

> This little book speaks volumes about self discovery as a prerequisite for vocation. Palmer takes you along on his life's journey and describes his struggles to recognize and use his own voice. His story is the search for authenticity and learning to be who you are and can become. In a thought-provoking and a very profound way, Palmer raises powerful questions to challenge your thinking as you do the "inner work" that is so important in preparing yourself for mentoring.

Emotional Intelligence at Work by H. Weisinger. (San Francisco: Jossey-Bass, 1998)

> The author's pragmatic and personal approach to emotional intelligence provides an easy explanation about how to make your emotions work for you by using them most productively. Three particular topics are noteworthy in light of mentoring: communication, interpersonal relationships, and the concept of an emotional mentor.

The Art of Possibility: Transforming Professional and Personal Life by B. Zander and R. S. Zander. (New York: Penguin Books, 2000)

> This is one of my favorite books. I give it as a gift frequently because I believe possibility is a precious gift. The Zanders present a dozen practices that will not only help you achieve your dreams but balance your life in the process—no easy feat.

Chapter 3: Finding and Getting to Know Your Mentor

Social Intelligence: The New Science of Success by K. Albrecht. (San Francisco: Jossey-Bass, 2006)

> In order to create a meaningful mentoring relationship you must work on and in the relationship. It takes social intelligence to do this successfully. As you read about Albrecht's model of social intelligence, the SPACE model, it will make you more acutely self-aware of what it is you need to do to make sure that you grow your mentoring relationship with your mentoring partner.

Make Your Connections Count! The Six-Step System to Build Your MegaNetwork by M. Giovagnoli. (Chicago: Dearborn Financial Publishing, 1994)

> Using your network to make your "net" work expands the pool of possibilities in selecting a mentor that is right for you. Giovagnoli makes building your connections a step-by-step process starting with discovering the contacts behind your contacts. Whether you are looking for a mentor or growing a business, the skill sets Giovagnoli lays out in this easy-to-read paperback are simple to follow.

The Career Navigation Handbook by C. Hunt and S. Scanlon. (San Francisco: John Wiley & Sons, 2004)

> If you are an executive considering choosing or changing careers you might use this resource to get started and position yourself. This book offers insights by executive recruiters who talk candidly about issues and trends in ten industries. If you are thinking about changing careers or choosing one, you will need a mentor to guide you. It is best to know about some of the issues and trends before you select one.

The Lost Art of Listening by M. P. Nichols. (New York: Guilford Press, 1995)

> Communication is a basic building block for establishing and maintaining a mentoring relationship. Listening is the bedrock for strengthening your communication skill. Nichols offers insights such as the difference between real dialogue and simply taking turns at talking; hearing what people mean, rather than simply what they say; dealing with defensiveness and differences of opinion; and understanding how the nature of a relationship affects listening.

Chapter 4: Establishing Agreements with Your Mentor

Relevance: Hitting Your Goals by Knowing What Matters by David Apgar. (Jossey-Bass, San Francisco, 2008)

> Apgar's book is a technical resource on how to strengthen your strategies for hitting your development targets. Apgar, an experienced business consultant, argues that failure to develop testable strategies and the difficulty of identifying relevant experience often lead to disappointing results. Apgar's four rules for how to develop workable strategies with relevant experience offer intriguing possibilities for dynamic mentor conversations.

The 4 Disciplines of Execution: The Secret to Getting Things Done, on Time, with Excellence by S. Covey and C. McChesney. [CD ROM] (New York: Franklin Covey Company, 2004)

Stephen Covey's four disciplines align well with the work of the nego-tiating phase of mentoring. Focusing on the wildly important (#1) is a pre-step in formulating initial or starter goals. It is from these that you identify the two or three SMART goals that would be most relevant to you mentoring relationship. The next discipline (#2) is to translate the lofty (starter) goals into specific actions. This is part of your work plan. The third discipline (#3) is to create a compelling scorecard (real-time measures of success). And finally, it is imperative is to build an accountability plan (#4). These imperatives are the four disciplines of execution and are as important to mentoring as they are to performance on the job.

The 3 Big Questions for a Frantic Family by P. Lencioni. (San Francisco: Jossey-Bass, 2008)

One of the most frequent goals that mentees struggle with is the chal-lenge of balancing work and family life. Through the lens of a simple fable, Lencioni provides a set of basic tools for "restoring sanity to the most important organization in your life," your family. Chances are you already know what good business practices look like, but have you ever thought about applying those same business practices to your life at home? Lencioni demonstrates how to take tried and true organiza-tional tools and apply them to balancing work and family.

The First 90 Days: Critical Success Strategies for New Leaders at All Levels by M. Watkins. (Boston: Harvard Business School Press, 2003)

The first ninety days in a new role are crucial to success. During those ninety days you need to get started, establish agreements, and execute on deliverables. As you've learned, the same is true in a mentoring relationship. Watkins offers ten strategies that are as applicable to your mentoring relationship and as to a new job.

Chapter 5: Doing the Work

The Power of Feedback by J. Folkman. (Hoboken, N.J.: John Wiley & Sons, 2006)

Most people don't know how to use feedback to really improve perfor-mance. Folkman has studied highly effective leaders and professionals and suggests that they treat and use feedback differently from most of us—they see feedback as a gift rather than a criticism, and they use it to focus and uncover strengths and work on doing a few things well. This book offers thirty-five concrete principles to help you turn feedback into real, effective, and long-term change.

Ongoing Feedback: How to Get It, How to Use It by K. Kirkland and S. Manoogian. (Greensboro, N.C.: Center for Creative Leadership, 1998)

> As a mentee, you need to be able to get the feedback you need and use it well. This little monograph drills down on feedback and provides additional tools and strategies to help you make feedback a personal habit and an ongoing part of your mentoring conversation.

Reaching Your Development Goals by C. D. McCauley and J. W. Martineau. (Greensboro, N.C.: Center for Creative Leadership, 1998)

> What I like about this learning resource is that it suggests various learning opportunities that you might use to further your mentoring goals. These suggestions can be used as a catalyst to brainstorm other learning opportunities that would be pertinent to you. It also has a list of questions you can use to think about other people who may be able to provide a support role in helping you reach your development goals.

Personal Styles and Effective Performance: Make Your Style Work for You by D. W. Merrill and R. H. Reid. (Boca Raton: CRC Press, 1999)

> The effectiveness of mentoring relationships is dependent on the ability to establish meaningful relationships. Merrill and Reid demonstrate how social behaviors—what an individual says and does—form exhibited and predictable patterns that can be identified and responded to. When these behaviors (driver, analytical, expressive, and amiable) are mutually understood, people are more likely to create productive and significant relationships as well as increase the quality of interaction and learning.

Crucial Conversations—Tools for Talking When Stakes Are High by K. Patterson, J. Grenny, R. McMillan, and A. Switzer. (New York: McGraw Hill, 2002)

> This is one of Lory's favorite resources to help mentors and mentees provide honest, straightforward, effective feedback and have conversations that seem difficult or are full of tension. It is easy to avoid dealing with difficult issues as a mentee, especially if you fear you might jeopardize an otherwise helpful relationship. The steps offered help mentees find an effective approach that avoids assumptions, defensiveness, and derailing. Stories from personal and professional life help you understand how to apply the principles.

Work a 4-Hour Day—Achieving Business Efficiency on Your Own Terms by A. K. Robertson and W. Proctor. (New York: William Morrow Company, 1994)

Motivational and business-time expert Robertson suggests that the priorities in our lives are often imposed by others. This book is more about how to rearrange your life to focus on personal and professional goals rather than focus on efficiency and working faster. This is a useful guide for recognizing and managing priorities and how to increase your persuasion and commitment to essential tasks and goals.

Chapter 6: Coming to Closure with Your Mentor

Words to Say Thank You by S. Hoggett and D. Fordham. (London: Cico Books, 2007)

I picked this book up at a conference and have since recommended it to many mentees. Although it is a little book, it is big on sayings, mottos, and phrases that anyone who wants to show appreciation can use. It is one of those inspirational little gifts that help you find the right words to express appreciation and gratitude to your mentoring partner.

Chapter 7: Making the Transition from Mentee to Mentor

Understanding and Facilitating Adult Learning: A Comprehensive Analysis of Principles and Effective Practices by S. D. Brookfield. (San Francisco: Jossey-Bass Publishers, 1986)

Effective facilitation is a basic process skill in the mentor's toolkit. Brookfield's in-depth description of the facilitation process and the six principles of effective practice he presents can help you make sure that the learning relationship stays on track. He offers examples and exercises that will stimulate your own reflection and assist you in helping mentees reflect on their learning processes.

Active Listening: Improve Your Ability to Listen and Lead by M. Hoppe. (Greensboro, N.C.: Center for Creative Leadership, 2006)

Most of us could improve our ability to listen. Since listening is so essential to mentoring, use as many resources as you can to improve your listening competency. This book includes quick and easy strategies for improving your listening skills along with tactical suggestions to raise your level of success.

Facilitator's Guide to Learning by D. Kolb. (Boston: Hay/McBer Training Resources Group, 2000)

One of the roles of a mentor is to be a facilitator of learning. This facilitator's guide is a companion to the Kolb Learning Style Inventory and an introduction to experiential learning theory and the instrument. It is chock-full of exercises that can inform your work with your mentee and includes technical specifications for the instrument itself.

Developing Adult Learners: Strategies for Teachers and Trainers by K. Taylor, C. Marienau, and M. Fiddler. (San Francisco: Jossey-Bass, 2000)

This volume melds theory and practice by presenting an array of field-tested learner-centric strategies for promoting adult learning and development. It includes seventy instructional activities from multiple practitioners in diverse practice contexts that focus on specific learning strategies such as collaborating, inquiring, visioning, and reflecting. These "how-to" strategies are useful as you work with your mentee.

The Mentor's Guide: Facilitating Effective Learning Relationships by L. J. Zachary. (San Francisco: Jossey-Bass, 2000)

After you've digested the topics in Chapter Seven, you may be ready to take a more in-depth look at the dynamics of the mentoring relationship. In *The Mentor's Guide,* I explore the four predictable phases of a mentoring relationship that make up the mentoring cycle and the key components of each phase. Like this book, *The Mentor's Guide* offers pages of templates, exercises, and tips to help you grow as a mentor and learn to steer the relationship in the most effective way to facilitate learning and growth.

REFERENCES

Albom, M. *Tuesdays with Morrie.* New York: Doubleday, 1997.

Albrecht, K. *Social Intelligence: The New Science of Success.* San Francisco: Jossey-Bass, 2006.

Apgar, D. *Relevance: Hitting Your Goals By Knowing What Matters.* San Francisco: Jossey-Bass, 2008.

Barnett, B. G., O'Mahony, F. R., and Matthews, R. J. *Reflective Practice: The Cornerstone for School Improvement.* Hawker Brownlow Education HB 3046, 2004.

Baugh, S. F., and Fagenson-Eland, E. A. "Formal Mentoring Programs." In B. R. Ragins and K. E. Kram (eds.), *The Handbook of Mentoring at Work: Theory, Research and Practice.* Thousand Oaks, CA: Sage, 2007.

Block, P. *The Empowered Manager: Positive Political Skills at Work.* San Francisco: Jossey-Bass, 1987.

Brookfield, S. D. *Understanding and Facilitating Adult Learning: A Comprehensive Analysis of Principles and Effective Practices.* San Francisco: Jossey-Bass, 1986.

Buckingham, M., and Clifton, D. O. *Now, Discover Your Strengths.* New York: The Free Press, 2001.

Cartwright, T., and Baldwin, D. *Communicating Your Vision.* Greensboro, NC: Center for Creative Leadership, 2006.

Cashman, K. *Awakening the Leader Within.* Hoboken, NJ: Wiley, 2003.

Collins, J. *Good to Great: Why Some Companies Make the Leap . . . and Others Don't.* New York: HarperCollins, 2001.

Covey, S., and McChesney, C. *The 4 Disciplines of Execution: The Secret to Getting Things Done, on Time, with Excellence.* [CD ROM.] New York: Franklin Covey Company, 2004.

Dalton, M. *Becoming a More Versatile Learner.* Greensboro, NC: Center for Creative Leadership, 1998.

DeLong, T. J., Gabarro, J. J., and Lees, R. J. "Why Mentoring Matters in a Hyper-competitive World." *Harvard Business Review* 2008, *8*(1), 115–121.

DiSilvestro, F. R. *Listening Dynamics Profile.* Bloomington, IN: Communication Dynamics Inc., 1996.

Edelman, M. W. *Lanterns: A Memoir of Mentors.* New York: HarperCollins, 2000.

Fischman, D. *The Secret of the Seven Seeds.* San Francisco: Jossey-Bass, 2006.

Folkman, J. *The Power of Feedback.* Hoboken, NJ: Wiley, 2006.

George, B., McLean, A., and Craig, N. *Finding Your True North—A Personal Guide.* San Francisco: Jossey-Bass, 2008.

Giovagnoli, M. *Make Your Connections Count! The Six-Step System to Build Your MegaNetwork.* Chicago: Dearborn Financial Publishing, 1994.

Hoggett, S., and Fordham, D. *Words to Say Thank You.* London: Cico Books, 2007.

Hoppe, M. *Active Listening: Improve Your Ability to Listen and Lead.* Greensboro, NC: Center for Creative Leadership, 2006.

Hunt C., and Scanlon, S. *The Career Navigation Handbook.* San Francisco: Wiley, 2004.

Kirkland, K., and Manoogian, S. *Ongoing Feedback: How to Get It, How to Use It.* Greensboro, NC: Center for Creative Leadership, 1998.

Klein, K. MentorNet 2008–Reprinted in MentorNet News [http://mentornet.net/documents/about/news/newsart.aspx?nid=35&sid=2]

Kolb, D. A. *Kolb Learning Style Inventory,* Version 3.1, 2008. [http://www.haygroup.com/tl/Questionnaires_Workbooks/Kolb_Learning_Style_Inventory.aspx]

Kolb, D. A. *The Kolb Learning Style Inventory* (version 3.1). Boston: Hay Group, 2005.

Kolb, D. *Facilitator's Guide to Learning.* Boston: Hay/McBer Training Resources Group, 2000.

Kroeger, O., and Thuesen, J. M. *Type Talk: The 16 Personality Types That Determine How We Live, Love, and Work.* New York: Tilden Press, 1988.

Knowles, M. *Self-Directed Learning: A Guide for Learners and Teachers.* Chicago: Follet, 1975.

Lencioni, P. *The 3 Big Questions for a Frantic Family.* San Francisco: Jossey-Bass, 2008.

McCauley, C. D., and Martineau, J. W. *Reaching Your Development Goals.* Greensboro, NC: Center for Creative Leadership, 1998.

McCullough, C. "Developing You!" *Training and Development,* 2007, *16*(12), 64–67.

Merrill, D. W., and Reid, R. H. *Personal Styles and Effective Performance: Make Your Style Work for You.* Boca Raton: CRC Press, 1999.

Nichols, M. P. *The Lost Art of Listening.* New York: Guilford Press. 1995.

Pace, T., with Jenkins, W. *Mentor: The Kid and the CEO.* Edmond, OK: MentorHope Publishing, 2007.

Palmer, P. J. *Let Your Life Speak: Listening for the Voice of Vocation.* San Francisco: Jossey-Bass, 2000.

Patterson, K., Grenny, J., McMillan, R., and Switzer, A. *Crucial Conversations—Tools for Talking When Stakes Are High.* New York: McGraw Hill, 2002.

Progoff, I. *At a Journal Workshop.* New York: Dialogue House, 1975.

Robertson, A. K., and Proctor, W. *Work a 4-Hour Day—Achieving Business Efficiency On Your Own Terms.* New York: William Morrow Company, 1994.

Taylor, K., Marienau, C., Fiddler, M. *Developing Adult Learners: Strategies for Teachers and Trainers.* San Francisco: Jossey-Bass, 2000.

Watkins, M. *The First 90 Days: Critical Success Strategies for New Leaders at All Levels.* Boston: Harvard Business School Press, 2003.

Weisinger, H. *Emotional Intelligence at Work.* San Francisco: Jossey-Bass, 1998.

Zachary, L. J. *The Mentor's Guide: Facilitating Effective Learning Relationships.* San Francisco: Jossey-Bass, 2000.

INDEX